The Wedding Catering Cookbook

Christie Katona

BRISTOL PUBLISHING ENTERPRISES
Hayward, California

A **nitty gritty**® cookbook

2005 Bristol Publishing Enterprises, 2714 McCone Ave., Hayward, CA 94545. World rights reserved. No part of this publication may be reproduced in any form, nor may it be stored in a retrieval system, transmitted, or otherwise copied for public or private use without prior written permission from the publisher.
Printed in the United States of America.
ISBN 1-55867-295-8

Cover design: Frank J. Paredes
Cover photography: John A. Benson
Food styling: Randy Mon
Illustrations: Caryn Leschen

Contents

Get Ready, Get Set, Go!

Cater Your own Wedding

More than most feasts, a wedding requires lots of advance planning, and every wedding is different. Because I have included instructions and suggestions for various different catering options, the book is not organized in a strict step-by-step fashion. However, many of my suggestions are geared toward a buffet-style reception, as this is both a manageable and flexible choice for a self-catered wedding feast.

I strongly encourage you to read through the front part of this book completely before you begin planning the food for your wedding. That way you can see which instructions and tips are most useful for your event. As there are so many things to remember, mark up the pages and sections which are helpful to you with yellow flags or highlighter.

My lifelong love of food and cooking was inherited from my grandmother, and nurtured by my mother who taught me the value of preparing wonderful meals for the ones you love. It brought me first to a classical training at the Cordon Bleu school in London, and finally to the world of catering, in which I have had the pleasure of providing food for over 800 weddings. While my menus are tailored specifically to suit each event, one aspect is common to all — the astronomical cost of catering meals for large groups of people. With my unique experience as a cookbook author, combined with my extensive background catering weddings, I knew I could easily help the budget-minded couple save at least half of the average reception cost simply by taking control of the food and drink preparation for that special day.

Behind every wedding couple are proud families and lots of caring friends who have watched bride and groom grow from child to adulthood. Who better than friends and family to help construct a memorable wedding feast made with love, for love? Coming together to prepare for the big day will provide much needed emotional support, bonding and will add extra warmth and great memories to the main event.

This can be a wonderful collaboration if you have a few friends willing to lend a helping hand with food preparation. Remember when friends or family help you should be extra appreciative of their efforts. For more challenging or work-intensive jobs, consider hiring appropriate catering staff. It's just a matter of logistics and delegation! So put your worries aside and get ready to have a great time!

Get Ready:

Assembling a Staff

The recipes in this book serve 50 people each. Expect to assemble a team of about 4 to 6 friends or helpers to cook a couple of recipes each, depending on how many guests you expect to serve. The rule of thumb for attendance at such events is generally that 75% of those invited will actually show up. Plan your menus accordingly.

You will need at least 1 helper, and preferably more than 2, for every 50 guests. Assign tasks to helpers, including setup, service and cleanup. If you prefer not to recruit friends for these tasks, try a staffing company which supplies restaurant jobs, or a local culinary school.

Important General Rules

- Assign a lead person to handle all details pertaining to the event. It is crucial that they have a list of all the times when activities are expected to take place, and names, phone numbers, and arrival times for all the vendors.

- Delegate! We usually have one person do the fruit and cheese display; another person can be in charge of the vegetables and salads; others can work on the main dishes and the breads and rolls.

- Put someone in charge of table linens, centerpieces, and getting the buffet set up. Whether you are using paper products or rental china, it takes a long time to get all the packages open and the room set up.

Site Requirements Checklist

Here is a reminder list of site requirements and considerations. You will need to think about at least some of these issues as you plan your wedding feast.

- Inside/outside: location affects planning
- Parking and security
- Duration of rental
- Plan for setup/cleanup
- Kitchen: refrigeration, oven(s)
- Ice machine
- Garbage disposal specifications
- Tables and chairs
- Floor plan
- Location of fuse box
- On-site management
- Key!

What About the Wedding Cake?

Although making your own cake falls outside the scope of this book, here are some helpful hints for purchasing and serving your cake.

- Visit bakeries and sample their cakes. Pictures may be wonderful but the taste may be uninspiring. Ask for recommendations from your friends and from caterers.

- Remember your budget: inquire about additional charges for delivery or return policy for cake items such as mirrors, stands, cake boards, pillars, drapery, etc.

- Be sure whoever is cutting the cake knows how and has a diagram for doing it properly. There is an art to disassembling a cake, getting the right portion size and ideal amount of icing on each piece.

- Some bakeries offer a variety of fillings and flavors in the same cake. It's nice for guests to have a choice.

- Not everyone likes sweets; it is not necessary to order cake for every guest. We have found that about 75% of the guests will have cake.

- Consider having just a small cake for the bride and groom and then offering a dessert bar to guests. Warehouse stores often have a great selection of desserts.

- If you are saving the top layer, place it on a heavy-duty paper plate or sheet of cardboard. Place it, unwrapped, in the freezer overnight. The next day, wrap it loosely in plastic wrap then tightly in heavy-duty foil. It won't be quite the same when you thaw it on your first anniversary, but it's the thought that counts.

- If you are using a cake top, have someone ensure that it gets home safely. Also, some brides and grooms use heirloom toasting goblets or cake knives and servers. Assign someone to look after these items—maybe the same person who looks after the cake top.

- If you are serving cake outdoors, make sure to inquire about the durability of the cake in hot weather. We have had cakes melt and slide, and squirrels do nibble.

- When photographing, make sure the cake isn't placed in front of a clock or windows, as they create glare.

- Place a cardboard box under the cake table so that when the person cutting cake removes pillars or other decorations there is somewhere to put them. Consider placing a damp bar towel on the edge of the box. That way the cake cutter can wipe their hands from time to time.

Cake Table Supplies Checklist

- tablecloth
- knife and server
- plates, forks, and napkins
- box for cake decorations and separators
- damp towel
- toasting goblets, Champagne on ice
- flowers for decorating

Cooking for Crowds

Getting Started

While most of us don't cook for hundreds of people every day, it really is quite manageable if you break the work up into segments.

- Shop for nonperishable items several weeks in advance. Although most of us keep items such as mustard, soda pop, and pickles in the refrigerator, many of these items can be moved temporarily into the garage.

- If you are serving cocktails, the ingredients can be purchased several weeks in advance. Punch ingredients can be bought at this time as well.

- I have found that my local drugstore carries a large variety of inexpensive wines. Warehouse stores, such as Costco and Sam's Club, are also great sources for beer and wine.

- Make sure you have proper storage containers as well as serving dishes for each item you will be preparing.

- Make sure you have adequate storage room in your refrigerator or freezer for the finished product.

- 13-gallon white plastic garbage bags are ideal for storing foods. They are also great for slipping over hotel pans (page 8) when transporting food.

Hotel Pans

Hotel pans, mentioned often in this book, are industry standard in food service and restaurants. They are 12 inches wide x 20 inches long and will fit in most home ovens. They are available in 3 depths: 2-inch, 4-inch and 8-inch. You can rent these pans. You can also purchase hotel pans made out of aluminum foil which work well and have the advantage of being disposable. If you are using a foil hotel pan and cooking a heavy item such as a turkey or ham, be sure you place it on a cookie sheet to give it added stability when moving.

Hotel Pan Yield

The chart on the next column shows some serving amounts for the hotel pan. You can always make portions larger or smaller, but this will give you some idea.

A 2-inch-deep hotel pan holds about $1\frac{1}{2}$ gallons of food; a 4-inch-deep hotel pan holds about $2\frac{1}{2}$ gallons of food.

Serving size	Number of servings per 2-inch pan	Number of servings per 4-inch pan
1 cup	24	40
$\frac{1}{2}$ cup	48	80
$\frac{1}{3}$ cup	72	120
$\frac{1}{4}$ cup	96	160

A #10 size can (a standard food service item) holds 12 cups, or 3 quarts, of food.

Hotel Pan Measurements

12 inches

20 inches

2 inches

4 inches

8 inches

Insulated Cookie Sheets

To prevent food from burning on the bottom, I like to use insulated cookie sheets. At our catering shop, we always have one on the bottom rack as a preventive measure. I have found the easiest way to clean messy hotel pans and cookie sheets is to spray them with oven cleaner. We are also fond of aluminum "scrubbies" to remove baked-on food.

Mixing Bowls

You will need very large mixing bowls to prepare food for a crowd.

Necessary Extras

- Be sure you have enough spoons, spatulas, sharp knives, measuring cups, paper towels, plastic wrap and foil.
- Keep a large supply of dish towels, aprons and pot holders ready.
- Clear off counter space and store appliances that won't be used in another room.

The Fabulous Food Processor

I cannot say enough good things about my Cuisinart food processor. I have used one extensively over the last thirty years. In the catering kitchen we have the largest model available and it is in constant use. I just can't imagine cooking without it! If you don't have one, it is definitely worth the investment. Be sure you read the instruction book thoroughly as there are a lot of different techniques to learn.

Be Flexible

About Cooking Times and Quantities

When you are preparing food for 50 guests or more, lots of basic cooking rules apply, but there are some changes related to the increased quantities. Please use your own judgment; for example, if you think something is cooking too long, test it three quarters of the way through the specified time. Then increase or decrease the cooking time as you see fit. Or if something is getting too brown, cover it with foil. Also keep in mind:

- Ovens vary greatly in their temperatures and the size of the pan used will make a difference.
- The times specified in the recipes will vary somewhat, according to the pans you use and the materials the pans are made from.
- The amounts of salad dressing required for the various salads are also a matter of personal taste.
- Taste frequently to make sure a recipe doesn't need more salt or garlic. We are fanatic about using freshly ground pepper in almost everything but desserts!
- If something is too thick, add more liquid.
- If something is too soupy, think about what you could add to the recipe to thicken it. Perhaps a bit more cheese or breadcrumbs would do the trick.

Think Big: Food Quantities

Here are some guidelines for purchasing food for 50 servings. Remember, it is always better to err on the side of too much rather than too little.

punch	3 gal. = fifty 8 oz. servings
coffee	1½ lb. + 2½ gal. water
crackers	2 lb.
rolls and butter	1 roll per person, plus 1½ lb. butter
salad dressing	1–2 qt., according to taste
potatoes	20 lb.
ice	14 lb. for chilling punch and ice water. You will need more for cocktails.
dried pasta	2½ lb. (for side dishes)
appetizers	12 per person for hors d'oeuvres, 6 per person before a meal
seafood	25 lb.
meat and poultry	25 lb.
salad	1 generous cup per person
vegetables	½ cup per person

Health and Safety

Here are some ironclad rules for keeping food safe and sanitary:

Always Wash Your Hands

- before you begin preparing food
- after you work with raw meat and poultry
- after you handle trash or garbage
- after using the restroom
- if you cough, sneeze or blow your nose
- if you touch your face, hair or body

Keep Food Fresh

- Wear disposable rubber gloves when preparing food.
- Keep food at correct, safe temperature.

- Bacteria and germs cannot grow if a food is colder than 45° or hotter than 140°.
- Always thaw food in the refrigerator or under cold running water: never let food thaw on the kitchen counter.
- Most of the recipes in this book are not hazardous as long as you use fresh ingredients, handle them with care and refrigerate them promptly.
- Most of us are aware that we would not leave a potato salad sitting in the sun for five hours and expect it to be nontoxic. Food served hot or cold should not sit at room temperature for more than 2 hours.
- Always have a bleach solution of 2 tbs. bleach + 2 gallons water in a container near at hand for wiping down surfaces.

Get Set:
Planning Menus and Service

Planning a menu that will appeal to a wide variety of guests requires consideration of many factors: the season of the year, the time of day, the age of the people being served and the type of occasion. A few other things to consider:

- Appetites tend to be heartier in colder weather; a main course of roast beef with roasted potatoes would be a good choice in December but much less so in August.

- If you are hosting an event at the dinner hour, your guests will expect a full meal, not just meat and cheese trays.

- Young men have big appetites, so be sure to allow for extra if you are feeding groomsmen! However, kids under ten seldom eat a full meal.

For our most basic dinner buffets we plan something like the menu on the next page. Additionally, offer 3 to 6 varieties of cheese and place them so if people are hungry before the meal is served, they can have something to nibble. As for sweet endings, wedding cake is usually the dessert of choice (see pages 3–5).

Getting More Elaborate

Using this menu as the foundation for a more elaborate meal, you may choose to feature additional offerings such as a choice of several hors d'oeuvres from which people can help themselves. Or add another entree or fish course, or another green or vegetable salad. During the winter months you may want to offer a fruited salad, such as *Ambrosia*, page 65, or *Honey Mustard Waldorf Salad*, page 92, instead of a fresh fruit display.

Basic Menu

Cheeses and Crackers

Main Meat*—chicken, roast beef or ham*

Starch*—potatoes, rice or pasta*

Green Salad

Rolls and Butter

Vegetables and Dip or Vegetable Item

Fresh Fruit Display

Dessert

Coffee, Ice Water and Punch

Plan Ahead

I t is very important to plan every aspect of your party in advance.

- Decide what to serve, then plan when and how to make it, how to store it and how to reheat it.

- Make lists for shopping, preparation and serving and check items off the list as they are accomplished; it will help everyone stay organized and focused.

- If your party will be in a rented facility, be sure that you tour the kitchen and make note of how to use any of the appliances that are unfamiliar to you.

- Avoid surprises by checking all appliances to make sure they work.

- Know the facility's rules for recycling and garbage disposal.

Deciding on the Menu

- When selecting a menu, consider a variety of foods — colors, textures, temperatures, flavor contrasts and rich foods as well as lighter foods.

- Sometimes guests have food allergies so it is imperative that you know what ingredients are in purchased foods. Peanut oil can be particularly bad for some folks and is often used in salad dressings. Shellfish is another item to be aware of. We take the precaution of printing out the menu and displaying it in a picture frame at the beginning of the buffet; this makes it easy for people to know if there is shrimp in the artichoke dip or anything else which may be a dietary concern.

Kitchen Set-Up

- Make sure your menu doesn't repeat items, such as spinach dip and spinach salad.
- Balance your menu with a selection of meat or poultry, fish or seafood, cheeses, vegetables and fruit.

Make sure someone will be on-site with a key to let you into the facility.

- Helpers should plan to be at the reception venue 3 hours ahead of the event.
- When helpers arrive at the kitchen, a "leader" should oversee setup.
- All cleaning supplies and towels go near the sink.
- Perishable foods go in the refrigerator.
- All ice goes in the freezer.
- Ovens should be turned on and heating.
- Make a time line and tape the time line and the menu to the wall for reference.
- Make a bussing tub full of sudsy water and place it by the sink. This will be used

Strapped for Cash Menu Option

The most time- and cash-efficient way to feed a large number of people and still have a lovely reception is to plan the wedding for early afternoon. That way people will have had lunch and you can just serve an assortment of appetizers and cake. A buffet of this type is much less expensive and manageable than a sit-down meal.

throughout the event to place utensils in as they get dirty.

- Make sure garbage cans are in place and have lots of liners available.
- Make sure there are lots of disposable gloves available for preparing food.
- Have a bleach solution for sanitizing — add 1 tablespoon bleach to 2 gallons water. Use this solution to wipe counters and sanitize surfaces.

Buffet and Cake Table Set Up

- Begin perking coffee.
- Set up coffee and punch table.
- Get a punch bowl ready for the water service.
- Have plenty of napkins and glasses on the table.

- The coffee and punch table is a good place to have nuts and mints.
- Make sure when an item is prepared and in its serving container, that there is adequate room in the refrigerator to store it.
- Prepare (but do not set out) creamer and sugar for coffee service. Place coffee cups where the coffee pot will go.
- Get the cake table ready with a cardboard box under it for storing cake decorations as cake is dismantled and served.
- Add cake knife and server, Champagne bucket and toasting goblets to the cake table. You will need to get forks, napkins and plates for the cake ready as well.
- If you are offering a carving station, place it at the end of the buffet. We use a large, wooden cutting board for that purpose.

On it we place a carving knife, fork, and a damp towel or two for wiping hands.

Bar Set-Up

- The bar setup should consist of the bar back, where beverages will be iced down and stored, and the bar front where drinks will be served. Make sure you have plenty of napkins, glasses and the necessary bar tools. You will also need a big clean bowl to fill with ice and a scoop to serve ice with if you plan to provide cocktails. See pages 22–27.

- It is important to keep a few of the empty beer and wine cases just in case not all of it is consumed. Then the wedding party will have something to put the leftover beverages in to transport them home.

- Do not open all wine or Champagne at once. Open as needed.

Last-Minute Tasks

- About 30 minutes before the event is scheduled to begin, go through the facility and make sure all is in order.

- Cheeses and crackers can be set out at this time, as well as breads and rolls. Be sure to cover them with napkins.

- Bring out creamer and sugar and make punch and ice water.

- Check on coffee and make sure it is brewed.

Buffet Presentation

People eat first with their eyes, so make sure your food is garnished and served on attractive serving ware.

- It is nice to have extra centerpieces on hand to place on the buffet, coffee and punch table, guest book table and also a centerpiece in the ladies' room.
- Vary the height of serving dishes by putting sturdy boxes on the buffet and covering them with linens or colorful overlays. It is easy to go to the fabric store and get some yardage in the color of your choice and add it to your buffet.

- If you are renting linens, a card table-sized linen makes an effective overlay. The size you should order is 54 inches square.
- If your facility allows them, candles are a wonderful way to make your buffet elegant. Hurricane holders or votives make them safe.
- If you are having more than 200 guests, you might want to think about having 2 identical buffets. No one likes to wait in line. Put the fruit centerpiece on the first table and place it perpendicular to the other tables. On that table place half of the plates, cutlery, and napkins on each side of the fruit. Then, about a 3-foot distance away, put 4 other tables – that is, 2 pairs of long tables, 6 or 8 feet each, parallel to each other to form a walkway

between. On those tables we start with the salad, then breads and rolls, vegetables, starch and main dishes. Having the main dishes at the end of the buffet makes people less likely to serve themselves too much food, and you less likely to run out of your main dishes! This layout works very well and really speeds things along.

Suggested Buffet Layout

Setting the Buffet

- If required, set up a carving station at the end of buffet.
- Make sure silverware, plates and napkins are available at beginning of buffet.
- Make a diagram of what goes where on the buffet and what utensils and serving pieces will be used to serve each item.
- Place serving utensils on buffet where the items will go.
- Assemble an attractive array of serving pieces such as baskets and platters well in advance of the event.
- Be careful not to have too many items that need to be spread or sliced at the buffet because the line will move too slowly.

- If offering salad greens, dress them just before placing them on the buffet to avoid delays and messy splashes.
- If offering a taco bar or baked potato station, separate it from the main buffet so those guests may help themselves at their leisure.
- For the average wedding reception we usually plan on 10 service tables. 1 for the cake, 1 for the gifts, 1 for the guest-book (this can be a smaller size), 1 for the coffee and punch, 1 for the music, 2 for the bar and 3 for the buffet.
- As a rule, unless it is a sit down dinner, you only need to provide seating for $3/4$ of your guests. You want some movement and flow for the reception, and not everyone will be seated all at the same time.

Garnishes and Presentation

I tell my staff it is against my religion to serve naked food! We are always careful about presentation.

- Use lots of fresh flowers, ferns and other greenery on the buffet. Be careful to rinse them well and check for bugs. Blot dry with paper towels and store in plastic bags in the refrigerator. Make sure any edible flowers you use were grown with no pesticides or chemicals, and that it is clear which flowers are to be eaten and which are just for looks.

- Use chive blossoms, mint leaves and sprigs of herbs such as thyme, tarragon, rosemary, basil, cilantro and parsley to make plates look fresh and pretty.

- Use fresh parsley, lemon slices, and purple kale leaves on buffet items.

- Garnishes bring freshness and color to everything they accompany, so use them liberally; you can't go wrong.

Beverage Service
And Alcohol at Your Reception

Most wedding receptions serve alcoholic beverages of some sort, the most common being beer, wine and Champagne. Champagne is most often served only for toasting. If you are not serving alcohol at your event, be sure to allow for extra coffee, punch and other beverages. You may of course choose to have a full bar or one serving only coffee and punch.

- Always provide a punch bowl filled with water and ice so that people can help themselves. Adding a few lemon slices and strawberries makes it pretty.

- If you are using a rental facility, know the rules regarding alcohol. Will you need an alcohol permit?

- It is perfectly acceptable to offer Champagne only for the toasting, and it is also acceptable to only offer one glass per person.

- Plan on serving about 75 drinks per case of Champagne.

- Usually Champagne is offered just prior to the cake cutting ceremony so that guests are ready to make a toast. It is also nice to have some sparkling cider on hand for those who do not drink.

- Bottled and canned beer is much easier to handle and serve than beer in kegs.

- A keg is less expensive but make sure you have a way to ice it down and that someone knows how to tap it. You will also need cups and pitchers for serving the beer.

- We have found that a new garbage can works well for holding kegs.
- You might want to invent a "designer cocktail" and name it after the couple.
- Some parties offer a selection of just two or three drinks, such as margaritas and screwdrivers or designer martinis. If that is your choice, it is a nice touch to print the selections offered on a plain white card and place it in a picture frame and have it sitting on the bar. Guests can quickly glance at the "drink menu" and make their choice.
- Consider making up large pitchers of the featured drink and have them ready to pour.

Basic Bar Equipment

- jigger, corkscrew, knife, ice scoop, bar towels
- pitcher of water
- large, attractive container for ice
- cut lemons and limes
- large plastic bins or ice chests to keep beer and wine cold
- Use an extra linen to cover up the more mundane items. With boxed wine, we remove the inner plastic liners holding the wine and put them directly on the ice so that the box won't dissolve. We then cover them with a table linen. This makes a much nicer presentation than having the boxes sit out.

If You Decide to Have a Full Bar

- It is difficult to judge the amounts of hard alcohol to buy for a bar. People vary widely in their tastes and consumption. The following list should serve as a suggestion.

Bar Shopping List

- 3 fifths each vodka, gin, scotch
- 2 fifths bourbon
- 1 fifth each blended whiskey, light rum, tequila
- 1 fifth each sweet vermouth and dry vermouth
- 10 bottles white wine
- 2 bottles red wine
- 1 medium-dry sherry
- 1 case each regular and light beer

Mixers

- 4 liters each club soda and tonic water
- 1 liter each ginger ale, 7-Up, cola, diet cola, bitter lemon
- 8 bags of ice, 7 lb. each
- bottled still water
- 1 quart each sour mix, Bloody Mary mix, orange, cranberry, tomato and grapefruit juices
- margarita mix
- grenadine
- liqueurs

Condiments and Garnishes

- 8 limes, 6 lemons and 1 orange
- cherries, olives and pearl onions
- celery sticks for Bloody Marys

Glassware

- 40 highball glasses
- 35 wine glasses
- 25 old-fashioned glasses

- Plan on one 7-pound bag of ice for every ten guests. You will need more in summer months or when you have a lot of beer and wine to ice down.
- It takes about an hour for a can a beer to chill in an ice bath, so be sure to allow plenty of time for your beverages to chill.
- If you are having more than 200 guests, it usually is easier and less work to call an ice company and have ice delivered. One client of mine had a cute idea that backfired — they put all their beverages in a fiberglass canoe out on the lawn. The weight of the ice and bottles caused the canoe to crack. I was certainly glad it wasn't my idea!

Liquor Liability

Be sure you use good sense when serving alcohol. Laws vary from state to state and guests are likely to overindulge when celebrating. You might want to check with your homeowner's insurance agent and consider getting an insurance "rider" for the day.

Always be ready to call a taxi or have another guest give someone a ride home. Have taxi service phone numbers at hand.

...Go!
Putting the pieces together

The day of the wedding is a hectic time, but proper choreography can counteract the overwhelming stress of putting all the pieces together.

Bridal Party

- Have food available for the bridal party before the wedding, something that is easy and clean, such as bagels and cream cheese.

- Beverages should be clear; liquids such as bottled water or 7-Up are ideal.

- After the wedding reception, pack a goodie bag of food, a bottle of wine and a couple of pieces of cake for the bride and groom to take with them on their honeymoon.

Children

Most wedding receptions do not have a lot of children in attendance. However, it is nice to have a special area designated for youngsters. You can even hire a babysitter to keep an eye on children.

- We recommend that you have an assortment of coloring books and crayons on hand, or little gift bags.

- Children usually do not eat much. We suggest that you have a kid-friendly item available for them to eat such as macaroni and cheese or hot dogs.

- Provide drink boxes for the kids; they are

less dangerous than a kid with a cup of punch!

When Guests Arrive at the Reception

- Make sure guests have a place to hang their coats.

- Employ a helper at the entrance to the reception to tell guests where to put gifts and cards. This person should also have a roll of tape to secure any cards that might go missing in action. A pen is handy to have as well, in case someone has forgotten to sign a card. This helper can also be in charge of the guest book. Usually a groomsman brings the guest book from the church to the reception.

- Perhaps most importantly, have the bar open and appetizers available without delay. This allows bride and groom to have last minute photos at the church or to take a bit longer for the limo ride while guests have some time to mingle and relax.

- When bride and groom arrive they can make a grand entrance and circulate for half an hour or so to greet guests.

Serve Dinner from the Buffet

When the meal is ready to be served, coordinate with the master of ceremonies or DJ to announce that the bride and groom will open the buffet, followed by the wedding party and their families. It is frustrating when guests try to begin the buffet before the bride and groom.

I hope you will find these tips helpful. Now let's get to the food!

Appetizers

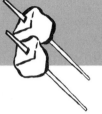

Mango Salsa

It is easy to use prepared salsa and make your own additions. To prepare a mango, stand it on end. Using a sharp knife, cut down each side of the large flat seed. You will have two halves. Make crosshatch marks approximately ½ inch apart through the flesh to the skin. Press center of halves, turning them inside out. Run a knife close to the skin to remove the mango flesh and you'll have perfect cubes.

1 bunch fresh cilantro, stems removed
1 bottle (54 oz.) prepared salsa
1 large red onion, chopped
4 mangoes, peeled and diced

Chop cilantro finely. Add to salsa in a large bowl along with red onion and mangoes. Stir until well combined and refrigerate in a covered container. Serve with tortilla chips.

Baked Crab Dip

This is rich and expensive and worth the indulgence.

3 lb. cream cheese, softened
1 cup half-and-half
2 tbs. Worcestershire sauce
1 cup chopped green onions
1 lb. crabmeat
1 cup sliced almonds

Heat oven to 350°. In a food processor workbowl or in a large bowl using an electric mixer, combine cream cheese with half-and-half until light and smooth. Add Worcestershire sauce and green onions. Transfer mixture to a large bowl. Carefully pick over crab for any cartilage. Gently stir crab into cream cheese mixture. Spread into a shallow, ovenproof serving dish which has been sprayed with nonstick cooking spray. Sprinkle with almonds and bake for 20 to 30 minutes. Serve warm with crackers, sliced baguettes or vegetables for dipping.

Artichoke Dip

Servings: 50

This is a favorite with everyone as there are so many variations. Here is a basic recipe and some of the most popular additions. Serve with crackers, sliced baguettes or tortilla chips. This dip can be made ahead and refrigerated for 48 hours covered with plastic wrap.

1 #10 size can (3 qt.) quartered artichoke hearts in water, drained
1½ lb. cream cheese, softened
2 cups mayonnaise
1 cup chopped white, red,or green onions
1 tbs. minced garlic
2 cups grated Parmesan cheese

Heat oven to 350°. In a food processor workbowl, coarsely chop artichoke hearts (or use a knife and a cutting board). Combine artichoke hearts, cream cheese, mayonnaise, onions, garlic and Parmesan in a large bowl until well mixed. Pour into a greased 4-quart casserole or 2-inch-deep hotel pan. Place an insulated cookie sheet on the middle rack of the oven. Place casserole on cookie sheet and bake for 1 hour, or until hot and bubbly.

Artichoke Dip Variations

- Add 2 cups cooked baby shrimp to dip.
- Add 2 cups crab to dip.
- Omit Parmesan. Add 3 cans chopped green chiles and dot with 3 cups of salsa. Swirl salsa through mixture using a knife (marble cake-fashion). Top with 2 cups shredded cheddar.
- Thaw two 8 oz. packages frozen chopped spinach. Squeeze moisture from spinach using a kitchen towel over the sink. Swirl spoonfuls of spinach into artichoke mixture and top with 2 cups prepared marinara sauce. Top with Parmesan.
- Stir 3 cups chopped water chestnuts and 2 packages Knorr Swiss vegetable soup mix, dry, into dip mixture. Add 2 packages frozen chopped spinach, as above.

Baked Brie

Servings:50

A large wheel of Brie cheese is always a hit on a buffet. It can be special ordered through the deli department at most grocery stores.

1 large wheel Brie, about 7 lb.

Heat oven to 350°. Place several sheets of foil crosswise on a cookie sheet to facilitate moving the cheese after it is baked. Also have several wide pancake turners or spatulas available.

Spread topping of your choice on Brie and bake for 20 to 30 minutes, or until cheese is warmed through. The sides of the cheese will start to curve outward when ready.

BRIE PRESENTATION

Macadamia-Berry Brie

3 cups raspberry jam

1 cup chopped macadamias

Before baking, spread jam in an even layer over cheese. Sprinkle a circle of nuts around the edge.

Apple Brandy Brie

3 cups peeled apples, cubed
1 cup brown sugar, packed

$\frac{1}{2}$ cup Kahlua liqueur or brandy
4 cups whole pecans, shelled

In a food processor workbowl, place apples; process until finely chopped. Stir in brown sugar and liqueur. Before baking, spread in an even layer on top of Brie and make a ring of pecan halves around the edge.

Honey Almond Brie

1 cup honey

1 cup sliced almonds

Before baking, spread Brie evenly with honey. Sprinkle entire surface with sliced almonds.

Brie Presentations

While baked Brie is delicious, there are other stunning presentations for this creamy cheese.
1 large wheel Brie cheese, about 7 lb.

Place Brie in the center of a platter or basket and try one of these ideas:

Brie in Aspic

Dissolve 1 package unflavored gelatin in ½ cup water until softened. Microwave for 30 seconds to melt and stir into 3 cups of white wine, such as Chablis. Let stand until syrupy. Using a pastry brush, apply a thin coat of the gelatin over the top of the cheese.

Place edible flowers and leaves in a pretty design over cheese. Purple pansies look fresh and dramatic against white cheese. Brush flowers and leaves with aspic to adhere to cheese. You may wish to give cheese several coats. Refrigerate until serving. Surround with strawberries.

Pesto-Style Brie Presentation

Make concentric circles with purchased pesto and chopped sun-dried tomatoes on the Brie. Scatter with pine nuts if desired.

Tapenade-Style Brie Presentation

Make *Olive Tapenade* (page 53) and spread in an even layer over Brie.

BLT Dip

Makes 1 quart

This delicious dip is great with pita crisps. To seed tomatoes, cut in half horizontally and gently squeeze out seeds over the sink. Remove stems and dice tomatoes into $1/2$ -inch pieces.

3 cups mayonnaise
3 cups sour cream
1 cup bacon bits
1 cup thinly sliced green onions
2 cups seeded and diced red tomatoes

Blend mayonnaise and sour cream together in a large bowl until smooth. Stir in bacon, onions and tomatoes. Cover and refrigerate.

Cheese and Chutney Spread

Servings: 50

The combination of flavors and textures in this appetizer make it a natural with Middle Eastern or Indian buffets. To determine the size of your mold, fill it with water and measure the water. Line the mold using cheesecloth or a damp tea towel (do not use terry cloth). Be sure to remove as much water as possible from the cloth.

1½ lb. cream cheese, softened
12 oz. shredded cheddar cheese
⅓ cup brandy or apple juice
3 tsp. curry powder

2 jars (8 oz. each) Major Grey brand chutney
1 bunch green onions, thinly sliced
1 cup slivered or sliced almonds, toasted

Combine cream cheese, cheddar and brandy in a food processor workbowl or in a large bowl using an electric mixer. Line a 6-cup mold with damp cheesecloth. Spread cheese mixture into mold, cover and refrigerate. Cut up any large pieces of fruit in the chutney. Heat chutney until warm in a small saucepan on low heat or in the microwave. Do not get the chutney too warm or it will melt the cheese. Unmold cheese onto a serving dish larger than the mold and with a rimmed edge. Just before serving pour chutney over the top of the cheese, letting it run down the sides. Scatter the green onions and toasted almonds over the top. Garnish with edible flowers and serve with crackers.

Cheese Display

With all the wonderful cheeses at the warehouse stores, the only problem is knowing when to stop! We usually offer about six varieties of cheeses on a cheese display. We cut some cheeses into cubes with a ripple cutter, others into wedges, some in slices and scatter the bright red wax-wrapped mini Goudas here and there.

Be sure to garnish your cheese display with edible flowers, grapes, and other fruits. This is an opportunity to really let your creative side show. Try scattering blueberries and edible blossoms over the cheese. In the winter, dried fruit and nuts can enhance your presentation.

Offer a basket of breads and/or crackers nearby to go with the display.

Chicken Wings

Chicken wings are a great item to serve on a buffet. Although there are a number of varieties preseasoned, here are some ideas for sauces of your own. Plan on four wings per person.

20 lb. chicken wings
salt and freshly ground pepper to taste

Heat oven to 375°. Spray two 2-inch-deep hotel pans with nonstick cooking spray. Thaw wings (if frozen) and spread in pans. Sprinkle with salt and pepper. Bake for 1 hour, turning occasionally to brown evenly. Drain off any excess fat. Combine sauce ingredients of your choice in a food processor workbowl or in a blender container; process until smooth. Pour over wings and continue baking for 20 to 30 minutes or until wings are glazed with sauce; stir occasionally.

Honey Soy Sauce

1 qt. honey
2 cups soy sauce
1 cup ketchup
½ cup salad oil
½ cup crushed garlic

Oriental Plum Sauce

1 qt. plum jam
1½ cups dark corn syrup
1½ cups soy sauce
½ cup crushed garlic
½ cup minced fresh ginger
½ cup finely chopped green onions

Spicy Apricot Sauce

1 qt. apricot jam
1½ cups ketchup
1½ cups cider vinegar
1 cup brown sugar, packed

½ cup soy sauce
½ cup crushed garlic
½ cup minced fresh ginger

.

For all sauce preparations, combine ingredients in a food processor workbowl and process until well blended. Refrigerate sauce if not using immediately

Deviled Eggs

Servings: 50

For a unique presentation, cut eggs in half, remove yolks and prepare filling. Arrange a layer of alfalfa sprouts on a large tray, place stuffed eggs in the sprouts and scatter edible purple pansies and violets among the eggs.

48 (four dozen) eggs

Place room-temperature eggs in a large pan of boiling water. Reduce heat to a simmer and cook for 12 minutes. Drain and rinse with cold water until eggs are no longer hot. Refrigerate eggs overnight. Peel eggs and cut in half. Remove yolks. Place yolks in a large bowl and add remaining filling ingredients. Mix until smooth.

All-American Filling

½ cup Dijon-style mustard
2 tbs. finely minced onion
1 tbs. lemon juice
4 dashes Tabasco sauce

enough mayonnaise to make a smooth
   paste, about 1 cup
salt and freshly ground pepper to taste
paprika or chopped fresh parsley, for garnish

Pesto Filling

½ cup prepared pesto
2 cloves minced garlic
enough mayonnaise to make a smooth
 paste, about 1 cup

salt and freshly ground pepper to taste
toasted pine nuts or chopped roasted red
 peppers, for garnish

Tarragon and Red Onion Filling

½ cup Dijon-style mustard
½ cup tarragon vinegar
½ cup finely minced red onion
salt and freshly ground pepper to taste

enough mayonnaise to make a smooth
 paste, about 1 cup
fresh tarragon sprigs, for garnish

Smoked Salmon Filling

1 cup finely chopped smoked salmon
½ cup finely chopped fresh dill
½ cup finely chopped capers

enough mayonnaise to make a smooth
 paste, about 1 cup
salt and freshly ground pepper to taste

Spoon filling into egg halves. Garnish as desired. Place on trays and refrigerate until serving.

Easy Bacon Dip

Servings: 50

Serve this with a variety of fresh vegetables.

3 cups mayonnaise
3 cups dry ranch dressing mix
3 cups sour cream
1½ cups grated Parmesan cheese
2 cups bacon bits

Combine all ingredients in a large bowl. Cover and refrigerate. May be made up to 48 hours in advance.

DIPS

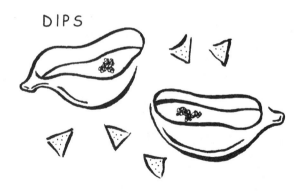

Easy Chili Dip

Servings: 50

This is so easy, it's embarrassing. You could also serve this at a Mexican buffet or at football parties.

1 #10 size can (3 qt.) chili con carne
1 pkg. (3 lb.) cream cheese, cut in chunks
1 can (12 oz.) chopped green chiles

Heat chili con carne and cream cheese together in a large heavy Dutch oven on medium heat, stirring occasionally, until cream cheese is melted. Stir in green chiles. Serve warm with tortilla chips.

Layered Shrimp Appetizer

This is so easy to make ahead. Rinse the shrimp before using them.

1 #10 size can (3 qt.) marinated artichoke hearts
12 eggs, hard-cooked
1 bunch green onions, thinly sliced
2½ lb cooked baby shrimp, rinsed and drained
3 cups mayonnaise
¼ cup lemon juice

Drain artichokes and reserve ¼ cup of the marinade. Coarsely chop artichoke hearts and place in the bottom of an attractive, shallow serving dish. Peel and chop hard-cooked eggs. Place on top of artichoke hearts and sprinkle with green onions. Layer evenly with shrimp. Combine mayonnaise with lemon juice and reserved artichoke marinade in a small bowl. Smooth evenly over the top of shrimp. Cover and refrigerate for up to 24 hours. Serve with crackers.

Meatball Basics

Servings:50

You will find a variety of cooked meatballs available at warehouse stores. Usually they come in 10-pound packages. This gives you 320 meatballs, about six meatballs apiece for 50 guests. Here are some sauces we like to use:

teriyaki sauce

Mr Yoshida's Original Gourmet Sauce

sweet and sour sauce

barbecue sauce

marinara sauce

Swedish Meatballs

4 cups sour cream

1 cup milk

1 tbs. minced garlic

1 tsp. allspice.

Heat oven to 350°. Combine sour cream, milk, garlic and allspice in a small bowl. Bake meatballs in hotel pans to heat through, about 30 minutes. Pour off any excess fat. Stir in sour cream sauce gently with a rubber spatula. The heat from the meatballs will warm the sauce sufficiently for serving.

Garnish the teriyaki and Yoshida's versions with pineapple cubes, diced green bell pepper and sesame seeds. The barbecue and marinara versions get a sprinkling of parsley.

Pesto Cheese Terrine

Servings: 50

This layered, molded appetizer spread can be made in your largest loaf pan. You can even use a shoe box to make a terrine! If you use a box, line it first with foil then with damp cheese-cloth or a linen tea towel.

3 lb. cream cheese, softened
2 cups prepared pesto
2 cups oil-packed, sun-dried tomatoes
black olives, sun-dried tomatoes and pine nuts, for garnish

Line a large loaf pan with damp cheesecloth. Combine cream cheese with pesto in a food processor workbowl. Process until evenly blended. Blot sun-dried tomatoes with a paper towel. Chop into 1/4-inch pieces. Smooth half of the cream cheese-pesto mixture into the bottom of the prepared pan. Top with sun-dried tomatoes. Smooth the remaining cream cheese mixture over the tomatoes. Cover and refrigerate at least overnight or for up to 48 hours.

To serve, remove cover from pan and place a serving tray on top of terrine. Turn over and remove mold and cheesecloth. Garnish with black olives, sun-dried tomatoes and pine nuts. Serve with crackers or sliced baguettes.

Pickled Antipasto

This is a delightful and low-calorie appetizer that is different and appealing.

Antipasto Marinade

1 qt. red wine vinegar
2 cups olive oil
1 cup water
½ cup sugar

1 tbs. minced garlic
1 tbs. salt
1 tbs. dried oregano
1 tsp. freshly ground pepper

Antipasto Vegetables

1 bag (3 lb.) cauliflower florets
5 lb. baby carrots

2 jars green olives with pimentos, drained
4 green bell peppers, cored and sliced

Combine vinegar, oil, water, sugar, garlic, salt, oregano and pepper in a large stockpot. Bring to a boil over medium heat. Check cauliflower to make sure the pieces are consistent. Add vegetables to marinade and cook for 5 minutes on low heat. Refrigerate vegetables in marinade for 24 hours. To serve, drain vegetables and serve on a rimmed platter. Try serving with sliced salami, cubes of provolone, and breadsticks.

Savory Cheesecake Squares

Servings: 50

These savory appetizers are rich, easy to prepare and feed a lot of people.

3 lb. cream cheese, softened
$1/2$ cup flour
12 eggs, beaten
3 cups sour cream

6 cups shredded cheddar cheese
2 cups chopped onion
2 cups cooked crumbled bacon
salt and freshly ground pepper to taste

Heat oven to 400°. In a food processor workbowl, combine cream cheese and flour. Process until smooth; add eggs and sour cream and process until blended. Transfer to a large bowl and stir in cheddar, onion, bacon and seasonings. Line two 13 x 9-inch baking pans with foil and spray with nonstick cooking spray. Divide mixture evenly between the 2 pans, smoothing tops with a spatula. Bake for 45 minutes. Refrigerate overnight. Remove from pans and cut into 1-inch squares.

- Pesto: use 2 cups pesto instead of onion, Parmesan instead of cheddar and chopped sun-dried tomatoes instead of bacon.

- Ham and Swiss: use Swiss cheese instead of cheddar, chopped ham instead of bacon.

- Goat Cheese: use goat cheese for cheddar; 1 cup chopped toasted walnuts instead of bacon.

Olive Tapenade

Servings: 50

This olive paste comes from Provence, France. It is delightful with pita bread, on crostini, as a topping for seafood or fish and as a dip for vegetables. It goes well with Mediterranean food, almost like an olive "salsa." The authentic recipe contains anchovies. They have been omitted here.

2 cups kalamata olives, pitted
2 cups oil-cured black olives, pitted
2 cups pitted black olives (niçoise, or any black olive)
1 tbs. minced garlic
1/2 cup capers, drained
2 tbs. lemon zest
1 tsp. crushed red chile flakes
1 cup olive oil

In a food processor workbowl, combine ingredients and pulse to make a finely chopped paste — do not puree. Cover and refrigerate. May be made up to 24 hours in advance.

Tuna Tartare

It is difficult to say how many people this will serve because some won't touch it and others will stand by the table and eat the whole thing. Be sure your tuna is sushi-grade and kept ice cold. We use ahi and albacore. Serve with crackers. Don't even try to make this without a food processor! Keep this dish very cold at all times.

2 lb. sushi-grade raw tuna, cubed
1 bunch fresh cilantro
1 small red onion. quartered
½ cup pickled ginger, drained

4 green onions, minced
2 tbs. sesame oil
1 tbs. chile oil
salt and freshly ground pepper to taste

In a food processor workbowl, pulse tuna until chopped — do not puree. Remove tuna and set aside in a large bowl. Remove stems from cilantro. In the food processor, pulse cilantro, onion and ginger until minced. Add to tuna and stir well. Add green onions, sesame oil, chile oil and season with salt and pepper. Adjust seasonings and refrigerate before serving. This can be made up to 8 hours in advance.

Honey Lamb Puffs

Makes 48

Lamb is one of my personal favorites. These little puffs are an attractive way to begin a Middle Eastern meal. It is helpful to start the lamb mixture a day ahead. When using puff pastry, it is important to keep the pastry cold and the oven hot. This will give the maximum "puff."

2 lb. ground lamb
2 cups onion, finely diced
2 tbs. minced garlic
salt and freshly ground pepper to taste
2 tsp. cinnamon

1/2 tsp. cayenne pepper
8 oz. tomato paste
1/2 cup honey
2 sheets puff pastry

In a large skillet over medium-high heat, cook lamb with onions and garlic until lamb is cooked through and onions are soft. Drain off fat. Season to taste with salt, pepper, cinnamon and cayenne. Add tomato paste and honey. Simmer for 10 minutes. Cool. (Filling may be made up to 24 hours in advance.) Heat oven to 375°. Spray mini-muffin pans with nonstick cooking spray. Using a sharp knife, cut puff pastry into 2-inch squares. Press into prepared pans. Spoon about 2 teaspoons of the lamb mixture into the center of each cup. Fold corners over to enclose lamb mixture. Bake for 15 to 20 minutes or until puffed and golden. May be made ahead and frozen unbaked. Do not thaw, just allow a bit more cooking time.

Smoked Salmon Presentation

Servings: 50

This is remarkably easy and delicious! We use mini bagels cut in half to go along with it; pumpernickel and rye bread are also favorites. To shave the onion, simply slice into paper-thin slices with a very sharp knife – or chop it into ¼-inch dice. I find that onions which are fat and wide are usually sweeter than those that are round. Use your prettiest platter and make this a masterpiece presentation.

2 sides smoked salmon
3 lb. cream cheese
1 jar (16 oz.) capers, drained
1 large red onion, shaved
4 tomatoes, seeded and chopped into ¼-inch dice
2 lemons, thinly sliced
crackers, bagels and breads for serving

Remove salmon from wrapping and place on the center of a beautiful tray. Place cream cheese in small bowls. Arrange cream cheese, capers, onion, tomatoes and lemon slices attractively around salmon. Cover and refrigerate until serving.

Shrimp Cocktail

Shrimp are always a big hit and it is almost impossible to buy too many. There are a plethora of sizes and preparations available at your warehouse store. We usually serve cooked, peeled and deveined large shrimp, 21/30 count — that is, 21 to 30 shrimp per pound. Thaw shrimp under cold running water and place them in large plastic bags. To serve, drain well and serve with cocktail sauce. Plan on 4 to 6 shrimp per person. To make them go farther, serve during the cocktail hour. Garnish with lemon slices and parsley.

200–300 large shrimp (about 10 lb.)

Easy Cocktail Sauce

Makes 1 quart

1 qt. ketchup
½ cup prepared horseradish
2 tbs. lemon juice

Whisk ingredients together in a large bowl. Place in a covered container and store in the refrigerator.

Sausage-Stuffed Mushrooms

Servings: 50

So many people come back into the kitchen and ask us for the recipe for these great mushrooms. They are not the prettiest things in the world, but they sure taste good!

2 cartons (40 oz. each) fresh mushrooms
3 lb. bulk breakfast sausage
1 large onion, chopped
2 lb. cream cheese, softened

1 cup sun-dried tomatoes in oil, drained and chopped
1 tbs. fennel seeds
1 cup grated Parmesan cheese

Heat oven to 350°. Wipe mushrooms clean with a damp towel. Remove stems and set aside. Place mushrooms stem side up on a large rimmed cookie sheet. In a large skillet over medium heat, brown sausage and drain off fat. Place reserved mushroom stems in a food processor workbowl and coarsely chop. Add mushroom stems and onion to sausage and cook until onion is soft. Cut cream cheese into small chunks and add to the sausage mixture, stirring to combine well. Add sun-dried tomatoes and fennel. Stir well. Scoop rounded tablespoonfuls of sausage mixture into mushroom caps, pressing firmly and mounding tops. Sprinkle with Parmesan. Bake for 15 to 25 minutes, or until cheese is melted and mushrooms are soft. Serve warm with plenty of napkins.

Roasted Corn and Black Bean Salsa

Roasting the corn kernels under the broiler really brings out the flavor in this salsa.

4 cups corn kernels
1 bottle (54 oz.) prepared salsa
1 bunch fresh cilantro, stemmed and chopped
1 large red onion, chopped
3 cups canned black beans, well rinsed and drained
2 avocados, peeled and chopped, optional

Heat broiler and spread corn on a rimmed cookie sheet. Broil for 10 to 15 minutes, stirring occasionally, or until corn is lightly browned. In a large bowl, combine salsa, cilantro, onion, beans and roasted corn. Add avocado if desired. Cover and refrigerate. Serve with tortilla chips.

Spinach Balls with Mustard Sauce Makes 50

These can be made ahead and frozen.

1 pkg. (3 lb.) frozen chopped spinach, thawed
1 pkg. (3 lb.) herb-seasoned stuffing mix
1 lb. Parmesan cheese, grated
1 tbs. minced garlic
6 eggs, beaten
1 cup (2 sticks) butter, softened

8 oz. cream cheese, softened
salt and freshly ground pepper to taste

2 cups mayonnaise
½ cup Dijon-style mustard
½ cup dry white wine

Heat oven to 350°. Place spinach in a kitchen towel and squeeze tightly over the sink to remove excess moisture. Place in a large bowl and combine with stuffing mix. Add cheese and garlic and mix well until thoroughly combined. Add eggs, butter and cream cheese and blend. Season with salt and pepper. If mixture is too dry, add another egg. Form into 1-inch balls. Place spinach balls on an ungreased cookie sheet. Bake for 10 minutes, or until piping hot and lightly browned. May be made ahead and frozen, unbaked, for up to 3 months. Thaw before baking. Serve with toothpicks and mustard sauce. For mustard sauce, combine mayonnaise, mustard and white wine in a small bowl and refrigerate.

Roasted Red Pepper Spread

Servings: 50

We like to use this mixture to stuff raw mushrooms. It's also great piped on an endive leaf for the holidays.

2 jars (15 oz. each) roasted red peppers
3 lb. cream cheese, softened
1 bunch green onions, thinly sliced
milk, if necessary
mushroom caps or endive leaves, optional
chopped fresh parsley or other herbs, for garnish

Drain roasted peppers and blot dry with paper towels. In a food processor workbowl or in a large bowl using an electric mixer, whip cream cheese until light. Add red peppers and onions and mix well. If mixture is too stiff, add milk to thin. Spoon or pipe mixture into raw mushroom caps or endive leaves. May also be used as a dip for fresh vegetables, just add more milk. Be sure to garnish with chopped parsley or fresh herbs.

Salads

About Vegetable Trays

Whether you call them "Veggies and Dip" or "Assorted Crudites with Dipping Sauce," fresh and lightly blanched vegetables are a popular choice for parties, and are good choices for weddings. Many vegetables can be purchased pre-cut and ready to add to your platter. I usually give them a rinse in cold water to refresh and then check them over for any overly large pieces or flaws. When choosing vegetables, I find carrots and cauliflower are the most popular. I try to balance an assortment of colors as well as some more unusual choices. Here are some suggestions for other good choices:

Asparagus
Snow peas
Sugar snap peas
Endive
Broccoli
Celery
Bell peppers: green, red, yellow and black
Cherry tomatoes

Grape tomatoes
Jicama
Mushrooms
Scallions
Zucchini
Yellow squash
Cucumbers
Radishes

Ambrosia

Servings: 50

Remember ambrosia salads? This old-fashioned favorite still appeals to all ages.

2 #10 size cans (3 qt. each) mandarin oranges, drained
2 #10 size cans (3 qt. each) pineapple tidbits, drained
1 jar (4 lb. 6 oz.) maraschino cherries
2 pkg. (16 oz. each) miniature marshmallows
2 pkg. (16 oz. each) flaked coconut
1 container (5 lb.) sour cream

Combine all ingredients in a large bowl, mixing thoroughly. Cover and refrigerate. This can be made up to 24 hours in advance.

Pea Salad

Servings: 50

Feel free to use your imagination as to what you like in your Pea Salad; this recipe is a good place to start.

1 pkg. (5 lb.) frozen peas, thawed
1 #10 size can (3 qt.) sliced water chestnuts, drained
1 bunch green onions, thinly sliced
1 can (16 oz.) bacon bits

1 qt. prepared ranch dressing
1 qt. sour cream
1 tsp. seasoning salt
tomato slices, for garnish, optional

In a large bowl, combine peas, water chestnuts and onions. Stir in bacon bits. In a separate bowl, combine ranch dressing, sour cream and seasoning salt. Add to pea mixture. Taste and adjust seasonings as desired. Store in a covered container in the refrigerator. May be made up to 48 hours in advance. Garnish with fresh sliced tomatoes, if desired.

Green Salad With Raspberry Vinaigrette

Servings: 50

It's really hard to let this vinaigrette recipe go — it is so unique and delicious.

2 pkg. (3 lb. each) field greens
1 #10 size can (3 qt.) mandarin oranges, drained

2 cups dried cranberries
2 cups crumbled feta or blue cheese
1 cup sliced almonds with skins

Raspberry Vinaigrette

1 tbs. minced garlic
2 tbs. Dijon-style mustard
1 cup balsamic vinegar
1 cup raspberry jam

2 cups salad oil
$\frac{1}{2}$–1 cup water, for thinning
salt and freshly ground pepper to taste

If making this in advance, place greens, oranges, cranberries, cheese and almonds in a 13-gallon white plastic bag. Store in the refrigerator for up to 24 hours. In a food processor work-bowl, process garlic, mustard and vinegar. Add jam and oil and blend well. If mixture is too thick, add water as needed. Add salt and pepper. Cover and refrigerate until serving.

Celery Seed Dressing Spinach Salad

Servings: 50

This salad goes well with chicken or pork. You can make the salad 24 hours in advance.

6 avocados, seeded, peeled and sliced
1 bucket (12 lb.) grapefruit segments
1 bucket (12 lb.) orange segments

2 bags (3 lb. each) fresh spinach
1 bunch green onions, thinly sliced
2 cups sliced almonds, toasted

Celery Seed Dressing

1 qt. salad oil
1½ cups sugar
1 cup cider vinegar
1 small onion, peeled and quartered

1 tbs. Dijon-style mustard
1 tbs. celery seed
1 tsp. salt
freshly ground pepper to taste

In a food processor workbowl or blender container, combine oil, sugar, vinegar, onion, mustard, celery seed, salt and pepper; pulse to blend. Pour into a covered container and refrigerate if not using immediately. Place avocados, grapefruit and oranges in ²/₃ of the dressing in the bottom of the salad bowl, or in a white plastic bag. Place spinach and green onions on top. Just before serving, toss salad, adding more dressing if needed. Sprinkle with toasted almonds.

As You Like It Potato Salad

Servings: 50

Everyone has a special potato salad recipe, but with prepared potato salad so reasonably priced, making it from scratch isn't necessary. Buy your favorite type at your discount store and add condiments as you wish.

3 containers (8 lb. each) potato salad

Add Any or All

4 cups diced celery

4 cups diced sweet or dill pickle

4 cups chopped sweet or green onions

4 cups sliced radishes

Garnish the bowl with purple kale, edible flowers, paprika and hard-cooked egg slices.

Other Good Additions

extra mayonnaise, mustard, sour cream or salad dressing for more tang
crumbled cooked bacon; chopped fresh herbs: parsley, dill, chives

Combine ingredients in a large bowl and season as desired. Store in a 13-gallon white plastic bag. Before serving, place in a large chilled bowl and garnish as desired.

Spinach Salad with Strawberries and Poppy Seed Dressing

Servings: 50

This dressing is also great on fresh fruit salad.

2 pkg. (3 lb. each) fresh spinach
1 flat strawberries, stemmed and sliced
1 #10 size can (3 qt.) mandarin oranges, drained
1 bunch green onions, thinly sliced

2 cups sliced almonds with skins on
4 avocados, pitted, seeded and diced, optional
Poppy Seed Dressing, page 71

Tear spinach into bite-sized pieces. Place in a large bowl. Add strawberries, oranges, onions and almonds. If using avocados, toss with a spoonful of the dressing to prevent discoloration. May be made up to 24 hours in advance and placed in a 13-gallon white plastic bag. Put the heavier ingredients on the bottom, such as the oranges and strawberries. Then place the spinach and nuts on top. Add the dressing just before serving. This salad is best served immediately.

Poppy Seed Dressing

1½ cups sugar
2 cups salad oil
⅔ cup cider vinegar
½ small white onion
2 tsp. dry mustard
2 tsp. salt
3 tbs. poppy seeds

In a food processor workbowl or blender container, combine dressing ingredients and process until thick. Pour into a covered container and refrigerate. Can be made several days in advance. Toss salad gently with dressing, taking care not to use too much dressing as this salad wilts easily.

Basic Pasta Salad

Servings: 50

We like to use sturdy, versatile penne pasta for most of our pasta dishes.

2½ lb. penne pasta, cooked and drained
1 qt. *Italian Dressing,* recipe follows
2 red onions, diced
1 #10 size can (3 qt.) pitted black olives, sliced
1 qt. cherry tomatoes, stems removed

1 #10 size can (3 qt.) marinated artichokes, drained
2 English cucumbers, halved and sliced
2 green bell peppers, chopped
1 lb. feta cheese, crumbled

Place pasta in a large bowl. Coat with *Italian Dressing* and add remaining ingredients, mixing well. Cover and refrigerate. This may be made 24 hours in advance.

Italian Dressing

2 tbs. crushed garlic
2 tsp. dried basil
1 tbs. salt
1 tbs. Dijon-style mustard

1 tsp. black pepper
3 cups salad oil
1 cup balsamic vinegar

Process all ingredients in a food processor workbowl. Refrigerate if not using immediately.

On Cooking Large Quantities of Pasta

Pasta will approximately double in volume after cooking, so be sure to use a big enough pasta pot. As a general rule, allow 1 gallon of water per pound of pasta. Add salt and a bit of salad oil to water to keep it from foaming. A 13-gallon pasta pot $2/3$ full of water takes almost an hour to bring to a boil. Slowly add pasta and bring it back to a boil. Cook about 4 pounds of pasta at once. You can turn the heat off and keep the lid on. Set a timer for 15 minutes and the pasta will cook perfectly. You don't have to worry about it boiling over, sticking or scorching. You do have to worry about carrying that heavy pot of hot water from the stove to the sink. Be careful and have your colander in the sink and a large container for the pasta nearby. Rinse pasta with cool, running water. For pasta salad, put cold dressing on salad to chill it faster. The pasta seems to absorb more flavor from the dressing. Just reserve a cup or so of the dressing to add just before serving. Store cooked pasta in a 13-gallon white plastic bag.

BLT Salad

To core and seed tomatoes, remove core with a sharp paring knife; cut in half horizontally, and squeeze gently to remove seeds.

12 heads romaine lettuce	1 can (16 oz.) bacon bits
12 tomatoes, cored and seeded	1 lb. Parmesan cheese, grated
2 bunches green onions, thinly sliced	1 pkg. (16 oz.) croutons

Tear romaine into bite-sized pieces. Chop tomatoes coarsely. Combine romaine, tomatoes, onions, bacon and cheese and toss with dressing. Refrigerate. Add croutons before serving.

BLT Dressing

2 cups olive oil	1 tbs. fresh mint leaves, or 1 tsp. dried
3/4 cup lemon juice	2 tsp. dried oregano
1/2 cup mayonnaise	freshly ground black pepper to taste
1 tbs. minced garlic	

Combine dressing ingredients in a food processor workbowl or a blender container; process until smooth. Pour into a covered container and refrigerate.

Broccoli and Raisin Salad

Servings: 50

This salad is always a big hit. You can vary the ingredients to suit your taste. We have found that using the food processor for the broccoli does not work, it makes the pieces too small.

2 bags (32 oz. bag) broccoli florets, chopped
2 cups red onions, finely chopped, or 2 cups green onions, thinly sliced
2 cups raisins or golden raisins
2 cups salted toasted sunflower seeds or salted chopped almonds
1 can (16 oz.) bacon bits
1 qt. prepared coleslaw dressing
salt and pepper to taste

Coarsely chop broccoli. Place in a large salad bowl and add onions, raisins, sunflower seeds, bacon and dressing. Stir well to combine. You may not want to use all the dressing. Season with salt and pepper. Store in a 13-gallon white plastic bag or covered container in the refrigerator. This salad may be made up to 48 hours in advance.

Cabbage Slaw with Shrimp

Servings: 50

To freshen up the taste of the shrimp, rinse in a colander with cold water and pick over for any pieces of shell. Place in a clean tea towel and give them a gentle squeeze to remove excess moisture. Sometimes I give them a squirt of fresh lemon juice to add flavor

2 pkg. (5 lb. each) coleslaw mix with carrots
2 bunches green onions, thinly sliced
2½ lb. cooked tiny salad shrimp (250–350 count per pound)

1 qt. prepared ranch dressing
2 tbs. fresh dill weed
salt and freshly ground pepper to taste

Combine ingredients in a large bowl. Adjust seasoning, if needed. Store in a 13-gallon white plastic bag. This salad goes well with salmon or a barbecue and can be made 24 hours in advance. Before serving, place in a chilled bowl and garnish with edible flowers or chive blossoms.

Chicken and Spinach Pasta Salad

Servings: 50

We got this recipe from a client many years ago and have been enjoying it ever since.

2 lb. bowtie pasta, cooked and drained
5 lb. cooked chicken strips
1 bag (3 lb.) fresh spinach
2 bunches green onions, thinly sliced
2 cups grated Parmesan
freshly ground black pepper
1 qt. prepared ranch dressing

Place pasta in a large bowl. Cut chicken into bite-sized pieces and add to pasta. Cut spinach into 1-inch strips using a sharp knife. Add to pasta mixture along with green onions, Parmesan, pepper and dressing. Mix well. Taste and adjust seasoning. May be made up to 24 hours in advance. Keep spinach separate and add to the salad just before serving.

Chicken Chutney Salad

Servings: 50

One of our most popular dishes for luncheons.

10 lb. cooked chicken
4 lb. seedless red flame grapes
1 #10 size can (3 qt.) pineapple chunks,
    drained

1 bunch celery, in ½-inch slices
1 lb. chopped macadamia nuts or almonds
1 bunch green onions, thinly sliced

Chutney Dressing

1 qt. mayonnaise
1 bottle (8 oz.) Major Grey chutney

1–2 tbs. curry powder

Cut chicken into bite-sized chunks and place in a large bowl. Add grapes, pineapple and celery. Combine mayonnaise, chutney and curry in a large bowl using an electric mixer. Pour over chicken mixture. Toss to thoroughly combine. Cover and refrigerate for up to 24 hours. Before serving, stir in nuts and onions.

Chop-Chop Salad

Add chicken strips to this salad for a main dish.

6 lb. iceberg lettuce, shredded

6 lb. romaine lettuce, torn into bite-sized
pieces

3 lb. shredded mozzarella

1 #10 size can (3 qt.) garbanzo beans,
rinsed and drained

1 #10 size can (3 qt.) sliced black olives,
drained

3 bunches green onions, thinly sliced

2 lb. diced salami, in ½-inch cubes

2 lb. plum tomatoes, seeded and diced

6 oz. fresh basil leaves, chopped

1 qt. *Italian Dressing*, page 72

Place lettuces in a large bowl. Add remaining ingredients and toss thoroughly. If making ahead, place lettuces in a 13-gallon white plastic bag and store in the refrigerator. Combine the rest of the ingredients in another 13-gallon white plastic bag and store separately in the refrigerator. Combine the two just before serving and toss with dressing.

Classic Caesar Salad

Servings: 50

Purchase hearts of romaine that are already trimmed and packaged. There are many good Caesar dressings available, as well as packaged croutons. Here are some interesting variations to try.

12 lb. romaine, in bite-sized pieces
1½ qt. prepared Caesar dressing
16 oz. seasoned croutons

1 lb. grated Parmesan
freshly ground black pepper

Pour dressing into a 13-gallon white plastic bag. Place salad greens on top of dressing. Add croutons, cheese and pepper. Place the bag in a bus tub or box to lend support. Refrigerate for up to 8 hours. Just before serving, shake bag well to evenly toss salad. Make sure bag is securely fastened.

Caesar Salad Variations

- Add cooked baby shrimp, grilled chicken strips or salmon for a heartier entrée.
- Use crushed tortilla chips and shredded cheddar instead of the croutons and Parmesan; add chopped red plum tomatoes and sliced black olives for a Mexican Caesar.

Pear and Blue Cheese Salad

Servings: 50

The flavor combinations and textures in this salad are wonderful. You could use shredded Gruyère cheese instead of the blue, for a change.

4 avocados, seeded, peeled and diced
4 firm pears, unpeeled, cored
2 pkg. (2½ lb. each) salad greens

2 cups hickory-smoked almonds
8–12 oz. blue cheese, crumbled

Dressing

1 tbs. crushed garlic
3 tbs. Dijon-style mustard
1 cup balsamic vinegar
2 cups salad oil

salt to taste
freshly ground black pepper
water, as needed

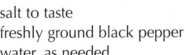

Place avocados in a large bowl. Cut pears into very thin slices and add to avocados. Prepare dressing by whisking together all ingredients in a large bowl. Pour dressing over avocados and pears to prevent them from darkening. Top with greens, almonds and cheese. Cover and refrigerate. Toss just before serving.

Crunchy Salad

Don't use a food processor to chop broccoli or cauliflower—it makes the pieces too small.

1 bag (3 lb.) broccoli
1 bag (3 lb.) cauliflower
1 can (16 oz.) bacon bits
2 red onions, diced

1 lb. raisins
2 lb. red flame grapes
2 cans (12 oz. each) Spanish peanuts

Chop broccoli and cauliflower coarsely. Place in a large bowl and add bacon, onions, raisins, grapes and peanuts.

Dressing

3 cups mayonnaise
1 cup cider vinegar
1 cup sugar

2 tsp. salt
freshly ground pepper to taste
dash of liquid smoke, optional

Combine dressing ingredients in a food processor workbowl; process until blended. Pour over prepared salad mixture and mix thoroughly. May be prepared 24 hours in advance. Add the peanuts just before serving.

Curried Rice Salad

Servings: 50

This is a great vegetarian dish. You can also add cooked baby shrimp or diced chicken for a heartier version. To speed up preparation we use a rice pilaf mix.

1 pkg. (40 oz.) rice pilaf mix
2 jars (9 oz. each) marinated artichokes
1 #10 size can (3 qt.) sliced water chestnuts, drained
1 qt. mayonnaise
4 green bell peppers, cored, seeded and diced

1 bunch celery, in ¼-inch slices
2 bunches green onions, chopped
1 cup chopped fresh parsley
1 cup green olives, drained and chopped
1 tbs. curry powder
salt and freshly ground pepper to taste
2 cups slivered almonds, toasted, optional

Prepare rice mix according to package directions and cool. Drain artichokes, reserving marinade. Coarsely chop artichokes. In a large bowl, combine rice, artichokes and water chestnuts. Stir in mayonnaise. Add bell peppers, celery, onions, parsley and olives to rice mixture. Sprinkle with curry, salt and pepper. Stir well, adding reserved artichoke marinade if mixture is too stiff. Add more seasoning if desired. Place in a 13-gallon white plastic bag or large container. Cover and refrigerate. This salad can be made up to 48 hours in advance. Correct seasoning before serving. Garnish with toasted almonds, if desired.

Romaine Salad and Bacon Dressing Servings: 50

This salad also works well using spinach instead of romaine.

2 pkg. (2 lb. each) romaine hearts
2 bunches green onions, thinly sliced
12 hard-cooked eggs, sliced
1 box (40 oz.) fresh mushrooms, sliced
1 can (16 oz.) crumbled cooked bacon
1 qt. *Bacon Dressing,* follows

Tear romaine hearts into bite-sized pieces. Add green onions, sliced eggs, mushrooms and bacon. Just before serving, toss with *Bacon Dressing*, page 85.

Bacon Dressing

1 lb. bacon, cut into $1/2$-inch pieces
1 onion, finely chopped
1 cup sugar
$1/2$ cup cider vinegar
$1^1/2$ cups water
3 cups mayonnaise

Fry bacon in a large skillet over medium heat until crisp. Remove from pan and drain on paper towels. Add onion to bacon drippings and cook until softened. Stir in sugar, vinegar and water. Bring to a boil. Remove from heat and cool to room temperature. Place mayonnaise in a large bowl, add cooled onion mixture and whisk to combine. Stir in bacon. Place in a covered container and refrigerate.

Blue Cheese and Walnut Beet Salad Servings: 50

Always rinse your walnuts in a sieve under running water to remove the residual skin. Blot the walnuts dry with a paper towel and bake on a cookie sheet at 350° for 8 to 10 minutes or until dry and light golden.

12 lb. beets
Cranberry Vinaigrette, recipe follows
2 lb. crumbled blue cheese
2 lb. toasted walnuts

Heat oven to 400°. Cut tops off beets and place on a large cookie sheet. Cover tightly with foil, sealing the edges well. Bake for 1 to 1½ hours until tender; they will feel soft when squeezed. Remove foil and cool beets to room temperature. Peel and cut into ¼-inch-thick slices. Arrange on a beautiful platter in concentric circles. Drizzle with *Cranberry Vinaigrette* and sprinkle with cheese and walnuts. Serve at room temperature.

Components of this recipe may be made up to 2 days ahead. Cover tightly and refrigerate. This is a stunning presentation garnished with orange or hot pink edible flowers.

Cranberry Vinaigrette

1½ cups apple cider vinegar
3 cups salad oil
¼ cup Dijon-style mustard
1 can (16 oz.) whole-berry cranberry sauce
1½ tsp. salt
1 tsp. freshly ground black pepper

Combine ingredients in a food processor workbowl and process until combined. Pour into a container and refrigerate.

Greek Salad

Servings: 50

I once was lucky enough to vacation in Greece; it's a magical place filled with history, beauty, sunshine and fantastic food.

10 lb. romaine hearts
3 English cucumbers
3 green bell peppers
1 large red onion

1 qt. cherry tomatoes
2 cups pitted kalamata olives, drained
1 lb. crumbled feta cheese
1½ qt. *Greek Dressing*, recipe follows

Cut romaine into bite-sized pieces and store in a 13-gallon white plastic bag in the refrigerator. Trim ends from the cucumber and halve them if they are large. Cut into ¼-inch slices using a ripple cutter, if desired. Core, seed and dice green peppers into ½-inch pieces. Slice red onion vertically into thin strips. Place the cucumbers, peppers, onion, tomatoes, olives and feta in a separate large storage container. Cover and place in the refrigerator. Can be prepared up to 24 hours in advance. Just before serving, toss romaine and vegetable mixture with the dressing to coat.

Greek Dressing

1 qt. extra-virgin olive oil
1½ cups red wine vinegar
½ cup lemon juice
1 cup honey
2 tbs. Dijon-style mustard
2 tbs. minced garlic

1 tsp. salt
1 tsp. freshly ground pepper
1 tbs. dried oregano
1 tbs. dried dill weed
1 tsp. dried mint

In a food processor workbowl, combine all ingredients and process until blended. Taste and adjust seasonings if desired. Store in a covered container in the refrigerator. This recipe may be made up to 1 week ahead.

Dilled Pea Salad

Servings: 50

This salad is colorful with lots of crunch. Be sure to thaw and drain peas well so they do not dilute the dressing.

1 pkg. (5 lb.) frozen peas, thawed
2 lb. cooked baby shrimp, rinsed well
1 bunch green onions, sliced
2 cups diced celery

1 qt. prepared ranch dressing
2 tbs. fresh dill weed
1 jar (12 oz.) roasted cashews

In a large bowl, combine peas, shrimp, onions and celery. Pour ranch dressing over the top and sprinkle with dill. Stir well to combine. Place in a 13-gallon white plastic bag or large storage container. Refrigerate. This salad can be made up to 48 hours in advance. Before serving add more dressing if needed, stir in cashews and pour into a large serving dish.

Autumn Chicken Salad

Servings: 50

This salad also makes a terrific filling for croissants.

1 lb. walnuts, coarsely chopped
10 lb. diced cooked chicken
2 lb. carrots
2 lb. apples with peel on

1 bunch celery, sliced
2 bunches green onions, thinly sliced
1 lb. currants, optional

Dressing

1 qt. mayonnaise
½ cup Dijon-style mustard

½ cup honey
1 tbs. Worcestershire sauce

Heat oven to 350°. Rinse walnuts in a colander under running water. Blot with paper towels. Toast walnuts on a cookie sheet for 10 to 12 minutes, stirring occasionally, until light golden brown. Cool. Place chicken in a large bowl. Shred carrots using the grating disc of a food processor or by hand. Repeat with apples, removing any large pieces of peel. Add to chicken with celery and green onions. Mix well. Add currants if desired. Mix dressing ingredients in a large bowl with a whisk. Add to chicken mixture and combine. This can be made 24 hours in advance. Just before serving add walnuts; taste to correct seasoning.

Honey Mustard Waldorf Salad

Servings: 50

This is a nice salad for fall served with chicken or pork.

4 cups water
1 tbs. lemon juice
8 lb. apples, cored and diced

2 lb. celery, sliced
1 lb. raisins or dried cranberries
½ lb. walnuts, toasted

Honey Mustard Dressing

2 cups mayonnaise
½ cup honey

½ cup Dijon-style mustard

In a large bowl, mix water and lemon juice. This will prevent the apples from darkening. Dice the apples into the water. Set aside while preparing remaining ingredients.

Combine mayonnaise, honey and mustard in a large salad bowl. Drain apples well. Stir apples, celery, raisins and walnuts into dressing. Cover and refrigerate for up to 24 hours.

Layered Salad

Servings: 50

This popular salad never seems to lose its appeal. Although it's not the most attractive presentation, I have found the most convenient way to make this salad is in a 4-inch-deep hotel pan. Fluff a colorful linen around the pan to disguise it.

5 heads iceberg lettuce
1 bunch green onions, thinly sliced
5 lb. frozen peas, thawed
2 bunches celery, sliced
1 #10 size can (3 qt.) sliced water chestnuts, drained
4 green bell peppers, diced

½ cup sugar
1 tbs. garlic powder
salt and freshly ground pepper to taste
1 qt. mayonnaise
4 cups grated Parmesan cheese
2 containers (6 oz. each) crumbled cooked bacon

Pound lettuce heads on the counter with the core facing down. This will loosen core so you can easily remove it. Cut lettuce into quarters and slice into 1-inch strips. Place in the bottom of a 4-inch-deep hotel pan. Sprinkle with green onions and peas. Add celery, water chestnuts and green pepper. Sprinkle evenly with sugar, garlic powder, salt and pepper. Spread mayonnaise on top. Top with Parmesan and bacon. Cover and refrigerate for 24 hours before serving.

Oriental Noodle Salad

Servings: 50

Feel free to add or delete vegetables as you wish.

4 lb. angel hair pasta
2 bunches green onions, thinly sliced
1 #10 size can (3 qt.) baby corn, drained
6 carrots, thinly sliced on the diagonal
6 red bell peppers, thinly sliced

1 #10 size can (3 qt.) sliced water chestnuts, drained
3 cucumbers, sliced lengthwise in half and seeded, then sliced on the diagonal

Cook pasta in boiling salted water until tender. Drain in a colander and rinse thoroughly. Place in a large bowl and add vegetables. Add dressing to coat.

Dressing

2 cups oil
1 cup rice vinegar
1 cup soy sauce
1/2 cup sugar

1/2 cup sesame oil
2 tsp. red chile flakes
1/2 cup toasted sesame seeds

Combine all ingredients in a food processor workbowl and process until blended. Store, covered, in the refrigerator. This salad can be made up to 48 hours ahead.

Oriental Ramen Salad

Servings: 50

I remember once we made this salad for 300 people at a church buffet and the lid fell off of the pepper –we called it Blackened Salad!

2 bags (5 lb. each) shredded cabbage with carrots

2 bunches green onions, thinly sliced

6 pkg. chicken-flavored Ramen noodles

1 cup toasted sesame seeds

2 cups toasted slivered almonds

Dressing

1 qt. salad oil

½ cup sesame oil

1 qt. rice vinegar

1 cup sugar

3 pkg. Top Ramen seasoning packets (discard others)

freshly ground pepper to taste

In a large bowl, combine cabbage and onions. Crush Ramen noodles using a rolling pin. Add to cabbage mixture. Combine oils, vinegar, sugar, contents of seasoning packets and pepper in a food processor workbowl; process until smooth. Add dressing to cabbage mixture. Sprinkle with sesame seeds and almonds before serving. May be made ahead and refrigerated overnight. Add dressing just before serving.

Spinach and Apple Salad

Servings: 50

Colorful and unusual, this nice salad is suitable to serve in the Fall or for Thanksgiving.

2 bags (2½ lb.each) fresh spinach
2 lb. fresh bean sprouts
2 jars (12 oz.each) marinated artichokes
6 red Delicious apples, halved and cored, not peeled
2 cups slivered almonds, toasted
2 cups grated Parmesan cheese, or to taste

Dressing

1 qt. salad oil
1 cup red wine vinegar
⅓ cup honey
2 tbs. Dijon-style mustard
1 tsp. salt
freshly ground pepper to taste
reserved marinade from artichokes

Tear spinach into bite-sized pieces. Rinse bean sprouts in a colander and blot dry. Drain artichokes, reserving marinade, and coarsely chop artichokes. Thinly slice apples and toss with a small amount of the reserved artichoke marinade to prevent discoloration.

In a large bowl in which you are going to serve the salad, place bean sprouts, artichokes and apples. Top with spinach, almonds and Parmesan. Cover tightly with plastic wrap and refrigerate. Just before serving, add dressing and toss to coat greens. Reserve any remaining dressing for another use.

Prepare dressing by combining oil, vinegar, honey, mustard, salt, pepper, and any remaining artichoke marinade in a food processor workbowl or a blender container. Process until smooth. Place in a covered container and refrigerate.

Entrees

Aloha Pig Roast

Servings: 50

A delicious recipe that tastes like the pig roasted in an Imu pit in Hawaii. Plan on at least 8 oz. of raw meat per person, as it cooks down considerably. As well as being a great wedding recipe, this is the perfect party entrée for a luau, and much simpler than roasting a whole pig.

25 lbs. boneless pork butt
½ cup minced garlic
½ cup minced fresh ginger
½ cup soy sauce
2 tbs. Worcestershire sauce
2 tbs. salt

Heat oven to 325°. Line two 4-inch-deep hotel pans with heavy-duty foil extending 15 inches over on each long side. Place the pork in the pans and sprinkle with garlic, ginger, soy sauce, Worcestershire and salt. Crimp the foil so that pork is sealed tight. Bake for 5 hours. Cool to room temperature.

Pour off fat and accumulated liquid. Shred meat into large chunks, discarding excess fat. Place meat back in pans and reheat for serving. Must be made ahead. Can be made 48 hours in advance, prepped and refrigerated in a covered container.

Baked King Salmon

Servings: 50

People love salmon and the warehouse clubs feature such wonderful salmon fillets. Try serving the salmon with Sour Cream Dill Sauce, *page 117, instead of the* Basil Butter.

12 lb. salmon fillets
seasoning salt for sprinkling

lemon pepper for sprinkling
½ cup fresh dill weed

Heat oven to 400°. Line half-sheet pans with foil. Place salmon on pans in 1 layer and sprinkle with seasoning salt, lemon pepper and dill. Bake for 15 to 20 minutes, or until salmon is just cooked through. Serve with Sun-Dried Tomato Basil Butter.

Sun-Dried Tomato Basil Butter

2 lb. butter, softened
1 cup sun-dried tomatoes in oil, drained

1 cup fresh basil, chopped
1 tbs. minced garlic

Combine ingredients in a food processor workbowl and pulse until blended. Cover and refrigerate until serving. This is also a great spread for crusty breads.

Baked Halibut with Sour Cream and Dill

Servings: 50

This is best prepared on-site just before serving. So be sure your facility has enough oven space to accommodate the number of trays you will need.

50 boneless, skinless halibut fillets
   (about 4 oz. each)
2 tbs. seasoning salt
2 tsp. white pepper

5 lb. sour cream
2 red onions, peeled and chopped
3 tbs. fresh dill weed

Heat oven to 350°. Line baking trays or half-sheet pans with foil. Place halibut in a single layer on baking pans and sprinkle with seasoning salt and pepper. Bake for 20 minutes or until fish is almost cooked through. While halibut is baking, place sour cream in a large bowl and beat until smooth using an electric mixer. Stir in onions and dill. Remove fish from oven and spread evenly with sour cream and dill sauce. Continue baking for 10 minutes or until topping is hot and fish is cooked through.

Brunch Strata

This is a wonderful make-ahead dish for a brunch. Italian sausage and Italian cheeses such as provolone, mozzarella and Parmesan work well. We slice some ripe tomatoes over the top during the last 10 minutes of baking and use a bit of basil in the eggs. Bellissimo!

2$\frac{1}{2}$ lb. bread, cut in cubes

9 lb. sausage, cooked, drained and
 crumbled

2$\frac{1}{2}$ lb. cheddar cheese, shredded

3$\frac{1}{2}$ dozen eggs, beaten

3 qt. milk

1$\frac{1}{2}$ tbs. dry mustard

salt and freshly ground pepper

Spray two 2-inch-deep hotel pans with nonstick cooking spray. Divide bread cubes evenly into the bottom of each pan. Divide sausage and cheddar evenly over bread cubes. In a large bowl, beat eggs (or divide ingredients between 2 bowls, if necessary). Add milk and seasonings. Pour over bread mixture. Cover and refrigerate overnight.

Heat oven to 325°. Place one pan on the center rack on an insulated cookie sheet and the other on the top rack. Bake stratas for 1 hour or until set. Cut into squares to serve.

Brunch Strata with Cranberries and Walnuts

Servings: 50

This easy brunch idea must be prepared the day before an event and baked just before serving. Serve with sliced ham, bacon or sausage along with fresh fruit and you are ready to go. Sometimes you can find liquid eggs that come frozen in half-gallon containers like milk cartons. They work well for recipes like this. Just thaw and follow the measuring advice on the carton. Find them at wholesale grocery stores.

3 dozen eggs, beaten
3 lb. cream cheese softened
1/2 gallon half-and-half
1/2 cup sugar
2 tbs. vanilla extract
2 loaves (1 1/2 lb. each) soft white bread, sliced
4 cups dried cranberries
1 cup chopped walnuts
Orange Syrup, recipe follows

Using a mixer, beat eggs and cream cheese in a large bowl till smooth. If your mixer is not large enough, divide mixture between 2 large bowls to complete recipe. Slowly beat in half-and-half until combined. Add sugar and vanilla. Spray two 2-inch-deep hotel pans with non-stick cooking spray. Layer each pan with bread, then cranberries and walnuts, then remaining bread. Pour half of cream cheese mixture over each pan of bread. With the back of a spoon or large spatula, press bread down into the egg mixture until all bread is soaked through. Cover with plastic wrap and refrigerate overnight. Place stratas in a cold oven, one on the center rack and the other on an insulated cookie sheet on the top rack. Heat oven to 325° and set timer for 30 minutes. Switch positions of stratas in the oven by moving the top to the center and the center to the top. Set timer for 20 minutes. Check stratas; they should be firm in the center and puffy. If needed, cook in additional 10-minute increments. Remove from oven and cut into squares. Each pan should have about 25 squares. Serve warm with *Orange Syrup,* below.

Orange Syrup

1 qt. orange marmalade	1 qt. orange juice

Heat marmalade and orange juice in a heavy saucepan over medium heat, until marmalade is melted and combined with juice. Serve warm over strata.

Chicken & Sour Cream Enchiladas Servings: 50

This is a really lazy version, but so good. Leave out the chicken if you wish. Some of the discount stores have packages of frozen, pulled chicken pieces which work beautifully in this recipe. Just thaw and cut any extra-large pieces into bite-sized chunks.

10 lb. cooked chicken, chopped
2 lb. thinly sliced green onions
5 lb. sour cream
2 cans (50 oz. each) cream of chicken soup

1 can (12 oz.) chopped green chiles
5 lb. shredded cheddar cheese, divided
5 lb. corn tortillas

In a large bowl, combine chicken and green onions. In a separate bowl, mix sour cream and chicken soup, and add to chicken. Stir in green chiles and half of cheese. Tear tortillas into 2-inch pieces. Add to sour cream mixture. Spray a 4-inch deep pan with nonstick cooking spray. Pour mixture into pan and top with remaining cheese. Cover and refrigerate. Can be made up to 48 hours in advance.

Heat oven to 350°. Place a cookie sheet under the enchilada pan. Uncover and bake 1½ to 2 hours or until bubbly and cooked through. If top gets too brown, cover loosely with foil.

Clam Spaghetti

Servings: 50

We have served this at church dinners featuring an Italian theme. The white sauce makes it a good choice for a wedding, as spills are less obvious.

5 lb. spaghetti
1 qt. olive oil
4 large onions, chopped
4 tbs. crushed red pepper flakes
1/2 cup minced garlic
1/2 cup dried basil

1/2 cup dried oregano
2 cups dry white wine
2 large cans (48 oz. each) chopped clams, drained, juice reserved
1 cup fresh chopped parsley
2 cups grated Parmesan cheese, divided

Place a large stockpot of water on high heat to boil. Place 2 large heavy skillets over medium-high heat. Add half of the olive oil and half of the onion, red pepper and garlic to each skillet. Cook for 20 minutes, stirring occasionally, to soften onion and season oil. Add basil, oregano and white wine, dividing between each skillet. Add spaghetti to boiling water in stockpot. Add clam juice, clams, parsley and 1/2 cup of the cheese to each skillet. Simmer until spaghetti is drained. Place spaghetti in a large bowl and add both skillets of the clam sauce. Toss well to combine. Top with remaining Parmesan. Serve immediately.

Jambalaya

Servings: 50

From your wholesale food source, it is possible to purchase both the rice mixes and 10-pound boxes of "pulled" chicken, both white and dark meat. If you are unable to obtain pulled chicken, just use 10 lb. of chicken tenders, baked and shredded.

6 pkg. Zatarain's Cajun rice mix assortment
10 lb. andouille sausage
5 lb. diced yellow onions
5 lb. diced celery
5 lb. diced green bell peppers
10 lb. pulled chicken pieces
1/2 cup minced garlic

1 #10 size can (3 qt.) whole tomatoes in juice
salt
freshly ground pepper
Cajun seasoning
cayenne pepper

Place the contents of 3 packages of rice mix and seasonings into each of two 4-inch-deep hotel pans. Cover with boiling water according to package directions. Seal pans tightly with foil and let sit for 1 hour. Heat oven to 350°. Cut sausage into 1/4-inch slices. Put in a 4-inch-deep hotel pan. Add onion, celery and peppers to pan. Bake for 1 hour, stirring occasionally. Sausage should be cooked through and vegetables tender. Pour off any excess grease.

Remove foil from rice and fluff with a fork. Divide sausage/vegetable mixture evenly between the 2 pans of rice. Add ½ of the chicken to each pan. Stir ¼ cup garlic into each pan, adding salt and freshly ground pepper to taste. Add Cajun seasoning and cayenne pepper as desired. Drain tomatoes and reserve juice. Coarsely chop tomatoes and stir into jambalaya. If mixture is too dry, add a bit of the reserved tomato juice. Garnish with parsley for serving. It is possible to make this up to 48 hours ahead, just be careful when reheating. You just want to heat the mixture through, not cook it additionally. Again, use the insulated cookie sheet trick. Place the cookie sheet on the middle rack of the oven.

Reheat Jambalaya at 300º for 30 minutes to 1 hour, stirring very gently every 15 minutes. Add water or more tomato juice if mixture becomes dry.

About Chicken Breasts

Without a doubt, chicken breasts are the most popular item to serve at receptions. They are easy to fix, everyone likes them and the portion control is already done for you. With all the varieties available at the warehouse stores, you need only check the package for the number of servings as most of the work is done for you. Here are some new ideas to try:

Chicken Piccata

Use cooked boneless, skinless breasts and sprinkle them with a bit of white wine, drained capers and lemon slices.

Italian-Style Chicken

Top cooked boneless, skinless breasts with seeded and chopped plum tomatoes, Parmesan cheese and slivers of fresh basil.

Sun-Dried Tomato Chicken

Use cooked boneless, skinless breasts and top with drained, oil-packed sun-dried tomatoes, crumbled feta cheese and toasted pine nuts.

Roast Beef with Horseradish Cream Sauce

Servings: 50

A carving station can be featured at the end of your buffet. Occasionally, people request prime rib but we find there is too much waste to make it work on the buffet line. Plus there is the added complication of doneness –from rare to well. We find that using a top sirloin, already cooked and vacuum-packed, is the best choice. All you have to do is unwrap the roast and heat it through. Allow for 4 servings per pound of roast beef.

12–13 lb. cooked roast beef, top sirloin preferred
4 cups sour cream
$1/2$ cup prepared horseradish
1 tbs. sugar
1 tbs. lemon juice

In a large bowl, combine sour cream, horseradish, sugar and lemon juice. Cover and refrigerate. You might want to add more horseradish if you like a zippier sauce. The sugar and lemon juice add complexity to the sauce, but feel free to leave them out.

Pork Loin with Mustard and Green Peppercorn Sauce

Servings: 50

You can use the seasoned pork loins available at warehouse stores, or use plain pork loin and season it yourself. Green peppercorns are available in most grocery stores next to the capers and condiments. Be careful lighting the brandy –I have set my hair on fire doing this!

20 lb. pork loin
10 whole cloves garlic, peeled
salt and freshly ground pepper

Heat oven to 325°. If not using seasoned pork loin, cut slits, ½ to 1 inch deep, into the pork with a sharp knife and insert garlic cloves deep into the meat. Sprinkle with salt and freshly ground pepper. Follow the directions on the package for cooking the pork loin. We usually bake several at once in 4-inch-deep hotel pans.

When pork is cooked, remove to a cutting board, tent loosely with foil and let rest while making sauce. Pour accumulated pork fat and juice into a large heavy skillet. Make sauce.

Mustard and Green Peppercorn Sauce

3/4 cup brandy or apple juice
2 cups whipping cream
1/2 cup Dijon-style mustard
1 jar (3.5 oz.) green peppercorns in brine, drained

In a large skillet, heat pork juices over medium-high heat until sizzling. Carefully add brandy and ignite with a long wooden match or lighter. (If using apple juice, do not ignite.) Shake pan carefully until flames die. Add whipping cream and bring to a boil. Cook, stirring, until mixture thickens. Add mustard and green peppercorns. Slice pork into 1-inch-thick slices and arrange on a platter for service. Drizzle sauce evenly overpork.

Turkey Dinner

Servings: 50

It is possible to purchase turkeys that have been boned and have the legs left on. They roast quickly and are easy to carve. Another alternative is to use a turkey breast, either boned or not. Oven roasting bags also work extremely well.

For whole raw turkeys, you will need 40 lb.
For a partially boned turkey, plan on 20 lb.
For a boneless roll, raw, you will need 18 lb.
For whole raw breasts, plan on 20 lb.

Cook turkey as per package instructions. Carve before serving and place on a large platter with *Cranberry Chutney* (see page 116) in the center.

If you can find it, LeGoux brand makes a wonderful canned turkey gravy — we swear by it. Serve with packaged mashed potato mix, adding cream cheese and milk to the recipe on the box.

Turkey Stuffing

You can buy wonderful bread stuffing mixes and then add your own personal touches.

6 lb. dry bread cubes
1½ tbs. poultry seasoning
1½ tbs. salt
1 tsp. freshly ground pepper
1 lb. butter

3 large onions, chopped
1 bunch celery, chopped
2½ qt. chicken broth
4 eggs

Heat oven to 350°. Cube bread and toss with seasoning, salt and pepper in a large bowl. Melt butter in a large skillet over medium heat. Add onions and celery and cook until softened. Add to bread cubes. Gently stir in chicken broth and eggs; do not overmix. Spray a 2-inch-deep hotel pan with nonstick cooking spray and add stuffing. Bake for 30 to 45 minutes.

Turkey Stuffing Additions

Add 3 finely chopped apples
Add 2 lb. cooked, drained and crumbled sausage
Replace ⅓ of the bread with 2 lb. crumbled cornbread
Add 2 cups toasted chopped pecans

Cranberry Chutney

Makes 12 cups

This is just the thing to serve with that turkey or roast pork.

2 cups water
8 cups fresh cranberries
2 cups raisins
2 cans (16 oz. each) crushed pineapple, drained
4 cups sugar
1 tsp. ground ginger
1 tsp. cinnamon
$\frac{1}{2}$ tsp. salt
$\frac{1}{2}$ tsp. allspice

Combine all ingredients in a large heavy saucepan. Cook over medium heat, stirring, until the cranberries burst and the mixture is thick. Place in a covered container and refrigerate. May be stored in the refrigerator for up to 1 month.

Sour Cream Dill Sauce

Servings: 50

Serve this with Baked King Salmon, *page 101, or with boneless chicken breasts.*

3 cups sour cream
1 English cucumber, finely diced
1 tbs. fresh dill weed
1 tbs. lemon juice
1 tsp. sugar

Combine all ingredients in a large bowl using a wire whisk. Cover and refrigerate. May be made up to 24 hours in advance.

Tip

After the wedding we always pack a goodie bag of food, a bottle of wine, and some wedding cake for the bride and groom to take away on their honeymoon.

Hurry Curry

Servings: 50

This is a great dish to serve for a tropical theme party. You can substitute shrimp or lamb for the chicken. The shrimp do not have to be cooked in advance as they will cook in the sauce. For ease of preparation, we often cook this recipe in two large skillets at once. Traditionally, curry is accompanied by rice and condiments, including chutney, chopped peanuts, sliced green onion, raisins, crumbled bacon, and shredded coconut.

1 lb. butter	2 cups flour
4 yellow onions, chopped	2 cups milk
1/4 cup curry powder	1 qt. unsweetened coconut milk
1 tbs. salt	4 qt. cooked, cubed chicken
1 tsp. white pepper	

Melt butter in a large skillet over medium heat. Stir in onion and cook until softened. Sprinkle with curry powder, salt, pepper and flour; stir to combine. Add milk and cook, stirring, until mixture is thickened and smooth. Reduce heat to low, stir in coconut milk and cook until the consistency of heavy cream. Do not boil. Add chicken and cook until heated through. Taste and adjust seasonings. If you like, add more curry.

Barbecue Pork Our Way

Servings: 50

This easy method produces a reasonable facsimile of the popular Chinese-restaurant-style barbecue pork. Serve with ketchup, toasted sesame seeds and mustard. Honey mustard is especially good for dipping and can be purchased at any warehouse store.

15 lb. pork loin	3 tbs. five-spice powder
2 cups sugar	2 tsp. salt
2/3 cup water	3 tbs. red food coloring
1/2 cup minced garlic	

Trim the pork of excess fat. Cut lengthwise into strips, about 2 inches thick by 3 inches wide. You can usually get three sections from each loin. Set pork aside. In a small bowl, combine sugar, water, garlic, five-spice, salt and food coloring to make a smooth sauce. Place pork in a 13-gallon white plastic bag and pour marinade over. Close bag and massage the marinade into the meat so that all surfaces are coated. Seal tightly and refrigerate overnight.

Heat oven to 350°. Spray 2-inch-deep hotel pans with nonstick cooking spray. Remove meat from marinade and drain. Place meat in pans (a close fit is okay). Bake for 1 hour, or until pork is cooked through. Cool for several hours in the refrigerator. To serve, slice meat on the diagonal. Arrange in overlapping slices on a large platter.

Side Dishes

Carrots with Fresh Ginger and Red Peppers

Servings: 50

This dish is colorful, flavorful and fresh-tasting.

15 lb. baby carrots
½ lb. (2 sticks) butter
6 red bell peppers, cored and seeded
½ cup fresh ginger, peeled and finely chopped
salt and freshly ground black pepper to taste

Steam or boil carrots until just tender-crisp. Drain well. Melt butter in a saucepan over medium heat. Slice peppers into thin (julienne) strips. Sauté in melted butter until softened. Add ginger and cook until ginger is limp. Stir peppers and ginger mixture into carrots. Add salt and black pepper to taste. Stir gently to combine. Serve hot.

May be made up to 48 hours in advance and refrigerated in a white plastic bag. To serve, heat for 10 to 15 minutes in the microwave.

Carrots with Grapes and Vodka
Servings: 50

Carrots are one of our favorite vegetables to fix for a crowd. They are sturdier than other vegetables and more tolerant of reheating.

3 bags (3 lb. each) baby carrots
1/2 lb. (2 sticks) butter
1 cup brown sugar, packed
1/2 cup cornstarch
1/2 cup vodka or apple juice
2 lb. red flame or green grapes

Steam or boil carrots until just tender-crisp. Drain well. Melt butter in a large saucepan over medium heat. Add brown sugar and stir until smooth. Stir cornstarch into vodka or apple juice. Add to the butter and brown sugar mixture and bring to a gentle boil. Stir in grapes and heat through. Pour grape mixture over warm carrots and stir gently to combine. Serve hot.

This dish may be made up to 48 hours in advance and refrigerated in a white plastic bag. To serve, heat for 10 to 15 minutes in a microwave, until hot. Check frequently and stir to rearrange carrots for even heating.

Corn Jumble

Servings: 50

This is a nice side dish for summer picnics. To seed a tomato, cut it in half horizontally and squeeze the seeds out over the sink.

5 lb. frozen corn, thawed
2 seedless cucumbers, peeled, in $\frac{1}{2}$-inch dice
1 red onion, diced
6 tomatoes, seeded and diced
1 qt. prepared ranch dressing

Combine corn, cucumbers, onion and tomatoes in a large bowl. Toss with dressing to coat. This dish can be made up to 12 hours in advance. Add dressing just before serving so that it does not become too watery.

Marinated Vegetables

Servings: 50

This zippy marinade makes a colorful, healthy offering on the buffet. Sometimes we add a #10 size can of pitted and drained black olives for even more color.

1 bag (3 lb.) broccoli florets
1 bag (3 lb.) baby carrots
1 bag (3 lb.) cauliflower

1 qt. cherry tomatoes or plum tomatoes
1 qt. large mushrooms, quartered through
   the cap

Vegetable Marinade

1 tbs. minced fresh garlic
4 cups cider vinegar
6 cups salad oil
1 cup sugar

3 tbs. fresh dill weed
2 tbs. salt
1 tbs. freshly ground pepper

Rinse vegetables and trim. Place in a 13-gallon white plastic bag or other container. Combine marinade ingredients in a food processor workbowl or blender container and process until blended. Pour over vegetables and mix well. Refrigerate at least 8 hours before serving. May be made up to 48 hours in advance.

Sweet Potatoes with Peaches and Cashews

Servings: 50

Here's something different for a holiday menu. The cashews make a crunchy counterpoint to the sweet potatoes and peaches.

2 #10 size cans (3 qt. each) sweet potatoes, drained
1 #10 size can (3 qt.) sliced freestone peaches, drained
1 cup brown sugar, packed
½ lb. (2 sticks) butter, softened
1 tsp. salt
1 tsp. ground ginger
2 cups cashews

Heat oven to 350°. Spray a 4-inch-deep hotel pan with nonstick cooking spray. Combine sweet potatoes and peaches and place in prepared pans. In a bowl, combine butter, sugar, salt and ginger. Sprinkle over top of potato mixture. Top with cashews. Bake for 45 minutes to 1 hour; until piping hot. This dish may be made up to 48 hours in advance.

Green Beans with Lemon Pepper

Servings: 50

It was a lucky day for us when we discovered how lemon pepper perks up the flavor of green beans. We all stood around in the kitchen gobbling platesful. To toast almonds, spread on a cookie sheet and bake in a 350° oven for 7 to 10 minutes. Stir occasionally and watch carefully so they don't burn.

4 pkg. (5 lb. each) fresh green beans (haricot verts are the best)
1 lb. butter, melted
2 tbs. lemon pepper, or to taste
salt
4 cups toasted almond slivers, optional

Cook beans until just tender in boiling water. Place in a colander and rinse with cold water until no longer hot. Place in a large bowl and add butter, lemon pepper to taste, salt to taste and almonds if desired. Place cooked green beans in a 13-gallon white plastic bag and refrigerate. This dish can be made 24 hours in advance. To reheat, divide mixture into 2 microwave-safe bags and heat in the microwave. Check every 5 minutes or until piping hot.

Baked Potato Casserole

Servings: 50

There are so many wonderful potato mixes on the market today, and they are a snap to prepare. Read the instructions carefully. Here is one of our favorite potato casseroles.

2 containers (5.5 lb. each) shredded instant
   hash browns
boiling water to reconstitute
2 cans (50 oz. each) cream of mushroom
   soup
2 cans (50 oz. each) of milk, as needed

1 qt. sour cream
3 lb. cheddar, shredded
1 bunch green onions, thinly sliced
1 can (16 oz.) bacon bits
freshly ground pepper
paprika, for garnish

Heat oven to 350°. Pour boiling water over potatoes in packages and let stand until reconstituted. Drain potatoes well in a colander. Place in a very large bowl and add soup, 2 soup cans of milk, sour cream, cheddar, onions, bacon and pepper. Pour mixture into a 4-inch-deep hotel pan that has been sprayed with nonstick cooking spray. Sprinkle top with paprika. (May be covered with plastic wrap at this point and refrigerated for up to 48 hours.) Put an insulated cookie sheet on the center rack of the oven. Place pan on cookie sheet and bake for 2 hours. Check to see that top is not getting too brown; if so, cover loosely with foil. Test center to make sure mixture is piping hot all the way through.

Roasted Garlic Mashed Potatoes

Servings: 50

It is possible to buy Roasted Garlic Mashed Potatoes *already prepared in plastic bags but they are rather pricey. This is a delicious and less expensive alternative.*

1 cup whole garlic cloves, peeled   ½ cup extra-virgin olive oil

Heat oven to 350°. Place garlic on a large square of foil. Coat with oil and bake for 30 minutes or until soft and golden. Cool to room temperature. Puree in a food processor workbowl.

1 box (2.4 lb.) instant mashed potatoes   1 qt. sour cream
boiling water   roasted garlic puree (see above)
1 lb. butter, softened   salt and freshly ground pepper to taste

Heat oven to 350°. Prepare instant potatoes with boiling water as directed, in a very large bowl. Mix with a wire whisk. Add butter, sour cream, garlic puree, salt and pepper to taste. Pour into a 4-inch-deep hotel pan that has been sprayed with nonstick cooking spray. (This may be covered with plastic wrap and refrigerated for up to 48 hours.) Place an insulated cookie sheet on the center rack of the oven. Place pan on cookie sheet and bake for 2 hours. Check to see that top is not getting too brown. If it is, cover loosely with foil. Test center to make sure mixture is heated through.

Sour Cream Potato Bake

Servings: 50

These are wonderful for a brunch or with baked ham for the holidays.

3 boxes (2.4 lb. each) shredded instant hash browns
boiling water for reconstituting
2 bunches green onions, thinly sliced
1 container (16 oz.) crumbled cooked bacon

5 lb. sour cream
2 cans (50 oz.each) cream of mushroom soup
5 lb. shredded cheddar cheese
milk to thin, as needed
salt and freshly ground pepper to taste

Pour boiling water over shredded potatoes in their open containers. Let stand for 30 minutes or until potatoes are tender. Drain well in a colander, pressing with the back of a large spoon to get the moisture out. Place in a large bowl and add onions, bacon, sour cream and soup. Add salt and pepper to taste. Add milk to reach a thick pudding consistency. Pour into a 4-inch-deep hotel pan which has been sprayed with nonstick cooking spray. Smooth top and garnish with remaining cheese. (Can be made 24 hours in advance. Cover and refrigerate.) Heat oven to 350°. Place a cookie sheet under the hotel pan to prevent bottom from overcooking. Bake uncovered for 1½ to 2 hours, or until piping hot when tested in the center. If top gets too brown, cover with foil.

Bread & Rolls with Ruffle Butter Servings: 50

Plan on 1 piece of bread or 1 roll per person. Serve Ruffle Butter *on a salad plate: on a large buffet it gets too messy. Plan on 1 plate per table of 8 guests. Ripple cutters are available at kitchen or restaurant supply stores. They are usually about 6 inches long.*

6 lb. butter plus ½ lb. on each table, or more according to your preference
fresh edible flowers or herbs (rose petals, pansies, chive blossoms, nasturtiums or other)

Make sure butter is very cold. Using a ripple cutter, slice butter crosswise into ½-inch slices. Place slices overlapping in the center of the plates. Scatter a small sprinkling of the flowers and/or herbs down the center of each portion. Refrigerate until serving. Make sure your refrigerator does not have a strong odor of garlic or onion as these cannot be covered.

A Word About Ham

The ever-popular, easy-to-fix favorite is a great choice for buffet dining. There is a large selection of wonderful hams at your warehouse store, particularly around holidays. We like boneless Pitt hams. Allow at least 15 pounds for 50 servings. Serve with *Baked Potato Casserole*, page 128, for a comfort-food dinner that your guests will love.

Couscous

Couscous is such a great food for serving to large groups of people. It's healthy, easy to fix and lends itself to a variety of preparations. This is one of my favorites and it's great to serve to clients asking for a vegan entrée (just leave out the butter). Always rinse walnuts under running water after chopping. Blot dry with paper towels and spread on a cookie sheet. Toast in a 350° oven for 10 to 20 minutes, until light golden brown. This really brings out the taste.

4 qt. hot cooked couscous (cook in chicken
   stock and white wine as on package)
1/2 cup (1 stick) butter, melted
3 cups green onions, finely sliced
1 cup chopped fresh parsley
2 cups currants

3 tsp. paprika
1 tsp. garlic chile oil
4 cups chopped toasted walnuts
2 tsp. salt
freshly ground pepper to taste

Place couscous in a large bowl and fluff with a fork. Add butter, onions, parsley, currants, paprika, oil, walnuts, salt and pepper and stir to combine. Serve immediately or at room temperature. May be made up to 48 hours in advance. Store in the refrigerator in a covered container or white plastic bag. To serve, bring to room temperature or warm in a microwave.

Mediterranean Couscous

Servings: 50

This can be used as a vegetarian or vegan entrée as well. Omit the cheese for vegans.

4 qt. cooked couscous
1 #10 size can (3 qt.) garbanzo beans, rinsed and drained
1 #10 size can (3 qt.) sliced pitted black olives, drained
1 lb. crumbled feta cheese
1 cup minced fresh parsley
2 cups *Italian Dressing*, page 72
2 tbs. Dijon-style mustard
1 tbs. grated lemon zest

Place couscous in a large bowl and fluff with a fork. Add garbanzo beans and olives. Stir in cheese and parsley. In a small bowl, stir together salad dressing, mustard and lemon zest. Toss with couscous mixture. Cover and refrigerate. This recipe may be made up to 24 hours in advance.

Baked Rice for 50

There are so many great things you can add to rice. Following this basic recipe are several ideas for easy, tasty variations depending on your preference.

3½ lb. rice
2 tbs. salt

4½ qt. boiling water

Heat oven to 350°. Rinse rice in a colander to remove starch. Place in a 2-inch-deep hotel pan. Add salt and water, stir well and cover with foil. Bake for 1 hour. Fluff with a fork.

Far East Style Rice

3 tbs. curry powder
toasted slivered almonds
½ cup (1 stick) butter

2 cups golden raisins
1 cup thinly sliced green onions

South of the Border Rice

3 tbs. taco seasoning
2 tsp. chili powder
2 tbs. minced garlic

2 cups each chopped onion, celery and
    green bell pepper

Classic Savory Rice

2 cups chopped onion sautéed in ½ cup (1 stick) butter
Stir in freshly parsley

Cooking Rice in Quantity

Rice is a lovely accompaniment to so many foods, chicken and fish especially. There are many wonderful rice mixes on the market and it is easy to purchase and prepare according to the package directions. We find that if you place the rice and seasonings in a hotel pan, add the salt and boiling water and then cover tightly with foil it will cook all by itself in about a half an hour. We have special Cambro (thermal food storage) containers for transporting which makes it even easier. If available, you can leave the rice in a very low oven, 300° or so, and check it after ½ hour. This is for the converted rice mixes as well as regular rice.

Mexican Rice with Black Beans

This is such a wonderful combination of flavors. It must be made ahead.

3½ lb. long-grain white rice

4½ qt. boiling water

Heat oven to 350°. Place rice in a 2-inch-deep hotel pan. Pour boiling water over rice in pan, stir and cover tightly with foil. Bake for 1 hour. Remove from oven and let stand for 5 minutes. Remove foil, fluff with a fork. Cool.

1 #10 size can (3 qt.) black beans, drained
2 lb. Monterey Jack cheese, shredded
2 lb. ricotta cheese
1 cup milk
4 red onions, diced

1 can (12 oz.) diced green chiles
¼ cup minced garlic
salt and freshly ground pepper to taste
1 lb. cheddar, shredded

Heat oven to 350°. Rinse black beans well in a colander under running cold water. Drain. In a large bowl combine rice and beans. In another bowl, mix Jack cheese, ricotta, and milk until blended. Add red onions, chiles and garlic. Combine beans and rice mixture with cheese mixture. Season with salt and freshly ground pepper. Spray a 4-inch-deep hotel pan with non-stick cooking spray. Pour mixture into pan and smooth top. Place casserole on center rack, place an insulated cookie sheet under the pan.

Bake for 45 minutes, until heated through. Top with cheddar and continue baking about 15 minutes longer until cheddar is melted and rice is piping hot. Casserole may be prepared up to 48 hours in advance. Cover and refrigerate before baking. Increase baking time by 10 minutes, as needed.

Sweets

Fruit Displays

Servings: 50

We have a custom-made acrylic fruit stand that is 3 feet high to display fruit. It makes a stunning presentation on the buffet. Think height when planning a fruit display. Put a stack of phone books on the buffet and drape them with a colorful overlay. Then place a large silver tray with an inverted bowl on top. Slice the bottom off a whole pineapple so that it will balance on top of the bowl. Place fresh flowers in the pineapple fronds and around the base of the bowl. Place clusters of grapes on the tray, then wedges of watermelon. Add slices of cantaloupe, kiwi, star fruit and whole strawberries among the other fruit. If you have more fruit than will fit on the tray, use several smaller trays flat on the table under the fruit display. Use more flowers to complete the arrangement.

2 fresh pineapples
12 lb. seedless red flame grapes
1 seedless watermelon
1 cantaloupe

3 star fruit (carambola), if available
6 kiwi
2 qt. strawberries

Have a bus tub, large towel, scissors and long sharp knife ready. Rinse all the fruit thoroughly under running cold water. You will be leaving the skins on. Use 1 pineapple as the centerpiece. Slice 1 inch off the bottom of the pineapple and the green fronds and 1 inch off the top of the pineapple. Stand pineapple on end and cut vertically in half. Cut each half lengthwise into thirds. Cut each wedge into 3/4-inch slices. Set aside in a large tub for building your display. Using scissors, cut the bunches of grapes into clusters. Set in tub. Using sharp knife, remove both ends from watermelon. Cut in half lengthwise. Cut into quarters lengthwise. Then cut into 3/4-inch wedges. Add to the tub. Place towel on table and place tub on it. Begin to build fruit display, placing in the center the whole pineapple, pineapple slices, grapes and melon slices on the tray as above. If more space is needed, add additional trays and place the rest of the pineapple, watermelon and grapes on them. Prepare remaining fruit and place in tub. Slice ends off star fruit and discard. Cut crosswise into slices. Repeat with kiwi. Rinse strawberries well, leaving tops on. Place the tub on the towel and complete fruit display. Garnish with flowers. In the winter months, when fresh fruit is not at its best, we find that grapes, pineapple, orange wedges and kiwi are still good. We intersperse the fruit display with cheeses, dried fruits, nuts and crackers for a more lavish effect.

Chocolate-Dipped Strawberries

Servings: 50

These glamorous treats are actually quite easy to make: the technique is more important than the recipe. They do not travel well, nor do they keep well. Make them about 3 hours before serving. It is important that you have enough refrigerator space reserved to chill them. Use an electric skillet for melting the chocolate, or a microwave. However, when melting chocolate in the microwave it will be necessary to reheat the chocolate from time to time as it cools down.

1 flat fresh strawberries
2 lb. semisweet chocolate chips

salad oil, about $\frac{1}{2}$ cup, as needed

Do not wash the strawberries or they will become soggy and the chocolate will not adhere. If they need it, blot gently with a damp paper towel. Heat chocolate in an electric skillet set at 300°. Stir when chocolate begins to melt; chips will begin to lose their shape and become glossy. Stir in a bit of oil to make a smooth mixture.

Prepare 3 or more cookie sheets lined with waxed paper or parchment paper. Hold a strawberry by green stem and dip $\frac{3}{4}$ of the berry into chocolate. Twist the berry as you remove it from chocolate and place on the prepared cookie sheet. Repeat.

It is difficult to say how many berries you can dip in this amount of chocolate as the sizes vary, as does the thickness of the chocolate. Sometimes after all the berries are dipped in semisweet chocolate, we melt a cup of white chocolate and a bit of salad oil. Then, using the tines of a regular fork, we quickly drizzle a zigzag pattern over the chocolate-dipped berries. It's really pretty and makes them look even more special.

You can also dip the warm chocolate-covered berries into finely chopped nuts or coconut. Using all white chocolate and white coconut is particularly fetching.

We usually serve these with the cake, placed on silver trays lined with white paper doilies. What could be a prettier garnish than a long-stemmed, red rose?

Tip: Coffee takes a while to brew!

Large coffeemakers take about an hour to perk, so be sure to allow plenty of time to make the coffee for the reception.

Chocolate Fondue

Servings: 50

The popularity of chocolate fondue inspired us to offer it at receptions. We serve this dessert in a pretty chafing dish and have one of our staff give each person a plastic glass with about a quarter-cup of the warm chocolate. We also supply long bamboo skewers and small plates.

1 #10 size can (3 qt.) hot fudge sauce

An Assortment of Fondue Dippers

pretzels
cake cubes
large marshmallows
strawberries

sliced bananas
dried apricots
cubes of pineapple
sliced pears or apples

Remove lid from fudge sauce and place can in a large saucepan. Fill pan with water $2/3$ of the way up the sides of the can. Place on medium heat and bring to a slow boil. Watch carefully and stir from time to time to prevent scorching. It will take about 30 minutes for the sauce to warm through. Pour sauce into a chafing dish to serve, and surround with platters of dippers. If using bananas, pears or apples, dip the slices in water with the juice of a lemon to keep them from turning brown.

Pumpkin Dessert

Servings: 50

This is rich, easy to make, and a perfect dessert for the holidays. If you are really in a baking mood, make the pie filling from scratch.

6 cans (16 oz. each) prepared pumpkin pie filling

2 boxes (1 lb. 2.25 oz. each) white or yellow cake mix

1 lb. butter, melted

2 cups chopped walnuts

whipped cream for serving

Heat oven to 350°. Spray a 2-inch-deep hotel pan or other large, shallow baking dish with nonstick cooking spray. Spread pumpkin pie filling evenly over the bottom of the pan. Sprinkle with the dry cake mix and drizzle evenly with melted butter. Top with chopped walnuts. Bake for 1 hour or until top is golden brown. Serve with a dollop of whipped cream.

Strawberry Shortcake

Servings: 50

This dessert is so easy, you almost don't need a recipe! To make it even easier, just use frozen, sweetened berries and canned whipped cream.

9 qt. fresh strawberries
2–3 cups sugar, to taste
7 vanilla pound cakes
1½ qt. whipping cream
1 cup confectioner's sugar
1 tbs. vanilla extract

Wash, drain and stem strawberries. Slice into a large bowl and add sugar to taste. May be prepared up to 24 hours ahead, covered and refrigerated. Slice each pound cake into 8 slices (you will have a few extra pieces to nibble on). In a very large bowl, using an electric mixer, whip cream until soft peaks form. Add confectioner's sugar and vanilla. To serve, top pound cake slices with berries, about ½ to ¾ cup for each serving. Top with whipped cream.

English Trifle

This dessert is lovely served in a silver or cut glass punch bowl. The amounts of ingredients can be varied to suit your personal taste. The wonderful butter-flavored pound cakes made in the bakery at your warehouse store make this quick and easy to prepare in advance.

6 loaf-sized, butter-flavored pound cakes
4 cups cream sherry
1 #10 size can (3 qt.) prepared vanilla pudding
2 bags (4 lb. each) mixed berries, strawberries, raspberries, or blueberries
1 qt. whipping cream
1 cup confectioner's sugar
1 tbs. vanilla extract

Cut pound cake into 1-inch cubes. Sprinkle with sherry. Begin by layering about a third of the pound cake, pudding, and berries into a large glass serving bowl. Repeat twice, using all the cake, pudding and berries. In a large bowl, using an electric mixer, whip cream until soft peaks form. Add confectioner's sugar and vanilla. Top trifle with whipped cream and refrigerate for several hours or overnight. Garnish with a few berries or edible flowers.

Minted Orange Sauce

Makes 50 servings

This is a lovely sauce to serve with fresh fruit.

3 cups sour cream
1 container (6 oz.) frozen orange juice concentrate , thawed
1 cup confectioner's sugar
1/2 cup finely chopped fresh mint

Combine all ingredients in a food processor workbowl; pulse to blend. Cover and refrigerate. May be made up to 24 hours in advance.

Index

Serve Creative, Easy, Nutritious Meals with **nitty gritty**® Cookbooks

1 or 2, Cooking for
100 Dynamite Desserts
9 x 13 Pan Cookbook
Bagels, Best
Barbecue Cookbook
Beer and Good Food
Blender Drinks
Bread Baking
New Bread Machine Cookbook
Bread Machine II
Bread Machine III
Bread Machine V
Bread Machine VI
Bread Machine, Entrees
Burger Bible
Cappuccino/Espresso
Casseroles
Chicken, Unbeatable
Chile Peppers
Clay, Cooking in
Coffee and Tea
Convection Oven

Cook-Ahead Cookbook
Crockery Pot, Extra-Special
Deep Fryer
Dehydrator Cookbook
Edible Gifts
Edible Pockets
Fabulous Fiber Cookery
Fondue and Hot Dips
Fondue, New International
Freezer, 'Fridge, Pantry
Garlic Cookbook
Grains, Cooking with
Healthy Cooking on Run
Ice Cream Maker
Indoor Grill, Cooking on
Italian Recipes
Juicer Book II
Kids, Cooking with Your
Kids, Healthy Snacks for
Loaf Pan, Recipes for
Low-Carb Recipes
No Salt No Sugar No Fat

Party Foods/Appetizers
Pasta Machine Cookbook
Pasta, Quick and Easy
Pinch of Time
Pizza, Best
Porcelain, Cooking in
Pressure Cooker, Recipes
Rice Cooker
Sandwich Maker
Simple Substitutions
Skillet, Sensational
Slow Cooking
Slow Cooker, Vegetarian
Soups and Stews
Soy & Tofu Recipes
Tapas Fantásticas
Toaster Oven Cookbook
Waffles & Pizzelles
Wedding Catering Cookbook
Wraps and Roll-Ups

"Millions of books sold—for more than 35 years"   **For a free catalog, call: Bristol Publishing Enterprises**
(800) 346-4889
www.bristolpublishing.com